Advancing the Oneness of Humanity:
The Olympic Games

Advancing the Oneness of Humanity: The Olympic Games

by

Kiser Barnes

GEORGE RONALD
OXFORD

George Ronald, *Publisher*
Oxford
www.grbooks.com

© Kiser Barnes 2024
All Rights Reserved

A catalogue record for this book is available
from the British Library

ISBN 978–0–85398–671–3

Cover design Steiner Graphics

Contents

Introduction — vii
Acknowledgements — xi

1. A Fixed Foundation for the Unification of Mankind — 1
2. Two Glorious Marathon Runs — 7
3. Nelson Évora (1984–) — 11
4. Religion and Sports: The Influence of Religious Values — 13
5. Of Vision and Action — 16
6. The Victory of the Covenant — 19
7. Striving 'Together' with Religious Values — 26
8. 'The greatest bestowal of God to man is the capacity to attain human virtues' — 29
9. A Team Victory — 32
10. Catherine 'Cathy' Freeman (1973–) — 38
11. Edward P. Hurt (1900–89) — 40
12. Matthew Bullock (1881–1972): Serving Human Oneness — 43
13. Unity in Freedom — 45
14. Harold Abrahams's (1899–1978) Race: A Run Beyond Class and Religion — 47
15. James Francis Thorpe (1887/8–1953) — 51

16 Betty Robinson (1911–99) and Other Pioneers	55
17 Prophetic Signs of Physical Valour	61
18 Eric Liddell's (1902–45) Run	63
19 The Unity of Mankind Will Be Achieved	67
20 Practical Measures for Human Oneness	69
21 Conclusion	76
Bibliography	79
References	87

Introduction

In November 1892 a 29-year-old French Baron, Pierre de Coubertin, stood before an audience in Paris to announce publicly an idea he had been formulating for many years. A passionate advocate for the power of sport to create moral and social strength, Coubertin cherished a dream to revive the Olympic Games of Ancient Greece in the modern era. He envisaged that a world-embracing sporting competition could serve to bring nations together and promote internationalism and peace.

Just six months earlier in that same year, Bahá'u'lláh – the Founder of the Bahá'í Faith – had passed away in the remote Ottoman penal colony of Acre on the eastern edge of the Mediterranean. Bahá'u'lláh had endured four decades of incarceration and harsh banishment at the hands of powers determined to extinguish His influence. Despite the probable lack of direct connection between Bahá'u'lláh and Coubertin – separated by more than 2000 miles and the paucity of reliable contemporary accounts that might have enlightened the Baron even further – one might today perceive in Coubertin's aspirations a sensitivity to the efflorescing spirit of the age that Bahá'ís believe was released into the world by Bahá'u'lláh's Revelation.

Coubertin's conviction that gathering athletes from different countries together for individual and group contests could help overcome prejudices and misunderstandings, aligned closely with Bahá'u'lláh's emphasis on the recognition of the oneness of humanity as the foundation to build world peace. The influential team of enlightened persons Coubertin put together saw the Olympics as an educational movement to cultivate nobility of character through sport; in like manner, the Bahá'í teachings view training as integral to individual and societal progress, emphasizing both spiritual and material education and faith in humanity's innate capacity for goodness and integrity. The Ancient Greek concept of calling a 'sacred truce' during the Olympic Games resonates with Bahá'u'lláh's prophetic vision of a future world order where humanity is able finally to set aside national, religious, and cultural boundaries to embrace an enduring sense of global citizenship.

It was also in Paris, in 1911, that 'Abdu'l-Bahá described how His Father Bahá'u'lláh had 'drawn the circle of unity'.

> He has made a design for the uniting of all the peoples, and for the gathering of them all under the shelter of the tent of universal unity.*

And that circle of unity – perhaps echoed in the five interlocking Olympic circles of unity – continues to welcome and encompass ever more diversity with every quadrennial Games. When the French capital hosted the second modern competition in 1900, women athletes were permitted to participate for the first time, with 22 women – out of 997 athletes – competing in five sports. In 2024 the 33rd Olympiad is the first Olympic Games with full gender parity on the field of play, also embracing ages ranging from an 11-year-old Chinese skateboarder to a 65-year-old Spanish equestrian. The participation of the Olympic Refugee team allows 37 athletes, displaced from their homelands, to compete on behalf of more than 100 million refugees around the world. The Paris 2024 Paralympic Games will engage more than 4000 athletes, each of them ready to make their distinctive contribution within the expanding circle of unity.

In 1911 'Abdu'l-Bahá foresaw that Paris 'will become a garden of roses! All kinds of beautiful flowers will spring up and flourish in this garden, and the fame of their fragrance and beauty will be spread in all lands.'† More than a century later,

---

* 'Abdu'l-Bahá, *Paris Talks*, p. 54.
† ibid. p. 169.

INTRODUCTION

the vision of unity in diversity is beamed across the planet from that same city to billions of television viewers. In his opening remarks at the 2024 games, Thomas Bach, President of the International Olympic Committee, told the assembled athletes:

> Now we are part of an event that unites the world in peace . . . In our Olympic world, we all belong.
>
> In a world torn apart by wars and conflicts, it is thanks to this solidarity that we can all come together . . .
>
> Let us celebrate this Olympic spirit of living life in peace, as the one and only humankind, united in all our diversity . . .
>
> Have faith in the future. Together, let us celebrate the best of our shared humanity.

The author of this publication, Kiser Barnes, has cherished a lifelong love of the Olympics. As an African-American growing up in strict segregated times, he would sit enthralled, watching the games on a small black-and-white television set, filled with pride when a black Olympian stepped out onto the track. The next morning, he recalls, the children of his neighbourhood would jubilantly race around, confident that they too would find their place on some winners' podium, somewhere in the future.

To all who admire the most impressive expressions of human capacity manifest in the participants in the modern Olympic Games and long for a world in which all are welcomed as equal members of one human family – where diversity, excellence and fellowship are celebrated – Kiser Barnes's thought-provoking and enlightening publication will serve as an inspiration.

Robert Weinberg
August 2024

Acknowledgements

I express deepest gratitude for opportunities to consider truths revealed in Bahá'í writings regarding some implications of the principle of the oneness of humanity in relationship to the Olympic Games. Fortunately, these efforts have involved ongoing learning and reflections, which has been enhanced by the assistance of many kind individuals. Without the loving support of my wife, Nancy Park, this book could not have been completed. She provided numerous forms of encouragement, as did my children, their spouses and my grandchildren – Demetris, Darrius, Lesaan, Keemia and Matias – whose love of sports I greatly enjoy.

I wish also to thank Jennifer Chingwe for her great assistance. She proofread the draft of the manuscript, reviewed and formatted the footnotes. She gave generously of her valuable and extremely limited time. The aid of the people at George Ronald – particularly Darren Smith, Managing Director, who supervised the book's publication, and Wendi Momen, who edited the manuscript into its final form – have been remarkable.

Baron Pierre de Coubertin

I

A Fixed Foundation for the Unification of Mankind

> ... establishing the divine religions
> has been the greatest means
> toward accomplishing the oneness of humanity.[1]

'The three values of olympism are *excellence, respect* and *friendship*. They constitute the foundation on which the olympic movement builds its activities to promote sport, culture and education with a view to building a better world.'[2]

The Olympics at Paris 26 July to 11 August 2024 was met with rousing excitement for its opening and closing ceremonies, its floating parade of national flags and Olympians in their uniforms. Its spectacular tapestry of about 326,000 spectators of different races, nationalities, ethnicities, genders, colours, classes and creeds showed its commitment to human diversity and oneness. Of the world's eight and a half billion people, an estimated four billion tuned in to portions of the broadcasted events. All of which indicated that the Games have an intrinsic spiritual value which appeals to all sorts of people.

Its charter, created by the father of the modern Olympic Games, Pierre de Coubertin, codified some of its values. First staged in Athens, Greece in 1896, the idea of establishing the modern Olympic Games as a means of establishing peace was envisioned by Coubertin. His awareness that the ancient games were 'primarily a spiritual affair' inspired him to action.[3]

Coubertin liked to declare that the Olympics was 'a display of manly virtues'. However, the 'goal of Olympism is to place sport at the service of the harmonious development of

*Stadium for the Olympic Games
Athens, 1896*

humankind, with a view to promoting a peaceful society concerned with the preservation of human dignity'.[4] This creates a culture in which everyone is equal in Olympic sport regardless of their background, gender, social status or beliefs.

Advancing its commitment for a harmonious and better world for humankind through the power of sports, this year in honour of International Women's Day on 8 March, the International Olympic Committee (IOC) distributed quota places equally to female and male athletes – 50:50. For the first time in Olympic history, an effort was made at Paris to achieve full gender parity on the field of play. It was a monumental leap forward.[5]

But more than that, in a new campaign film, distributed before the Olympic Games began, the President of the IOC, Thomas Bach, declared: 'Sport is at the heart of the Olympic Games. But they are about so much more than that. They go beyond competition. They are about living the Olympic values, about feeling the emotions, about enjoying the opportunities, about sharing wonderful memories. This is the unique and enduring spirit of the Olympic Games that we are about to witness at Paris 2024, and beyond.'[6] And the world enjoyed witnessing it.

Unity of Thought in World Undertakings

The Olympics' progressive and successive achievement underscores the conviction that the modern Games represent an aspect of that expanding 'unity of thought in world undertakings',[7] which the Bahá'í writings suggest nations will achieve as one of those 'candles of unity' (sources of light and direction) illuminating, in the metaphorical language of religion, the way towards human oneness. This 'candle' is considered below, along with other 'candles'.

An even century ago, the Paris Games featured the first elaborate nations' opening ceremony. The 1924 Games were considered remarkable at the time, and, 'in retrospect, marked a hinge point in the Olympic movement'.[8] Some transformative moments from the 1924 Games are highlighted below, along with other Olympics experiences, and some Bahá'í teachings and experiences. All these offer profound appreciations not only for the world's rich human diversity, but for the very oneness of humanity.

The Symbolic Character of the Olympic Games

Let us first recall that Coubertin believed,

> There is a need for something else besides athleticism and sport. We want the presence of national genius, the collaboration of the Muses, the cult of beauty, all the display pertaining to the strong symbolism incarnate in the past by the Olympic Games and which must continue to be represented in our modern times.[9]

The Olympics' symbolic flame and its interlocked rings representing the five continents have made the quadrennial spectacle a magnificent example of human oneness. The world's acceptance of these symbols constitutes an outstanding breakthrough for Olympism, a world festival for humanity larger than the glory of race, ethnicity, gender, nationalism and other identifications.[10]

The five intertwined rings of blue, yellow, black, green and red represent five continents. The five colours were chosen so that in combination with the white background they could produce the colours of all national flags worldwide but do not represent any particular continent. They symbolize the unification of the nations, which Coubertin envisaged the modern Games could help promote.[11]

The flame recalls the myth of Prometheus, the Greek demi-god, who gave fire to humans so that they could prepare food, and vanquish cold and darkness. It represents a lighting of the way for an upright life. It was at the Games in Berlin 1936 that the Olympic flame was lit for the first time during the spectacular opening ceremony.

A large measure of affection for the latest Games was, of course, the rare opportunities provided to witness some 10,500 male and female world-class athletes from 206 nations striving in 329 medal contests to win medals for themselves, their nations, their peoples, with great flings of energy, with grace and poise, with courage and heart, and more, which peoples from every background love. Athletes vied together symbolically, one could say, for the oneness of humanity. And no matter how long those Games exist, there will be great athletes to cheer and learn from. There will likely be a little girl or woman who will tumble the length of a balance beam, and in one perfect performance achieve a transcendent greatness that will live forever in the hearts.

From a Bahá'í perspective, it seems important to appreciate that all the athletic virtues exhibited in the Games underscore the following statements: 'The greatest bestowal of God to man is the capacity to attain human virtues.'[12] 'It is religion . . . which produces all human virtues, and it is these virtues which are the bright candles of civilization.'[13] '. . . the religion of God remains . . . that fixed foundation which insures the progress . . . of humanity. It has ever been the cause of . . . true fellowship and unification of all mankind'.[14]

The springboards for considering that the Olympic Games foster a sense of an emerging, united world which embraces human variety and a shared human heritage, in relationship to the principle of the oneness of humanity, are teachings of the Bahá'í Faith. Its writings hold that 'Every age requires a central impetus or movement.' And in response to the question, 'What is the spirit of this age, what is its focal point?', its writings proclaim, 'It is the establishment of Universal Peace, the establishment of the knowledge that humanity is one family.'[15] It is the reality of 'the oneness of the human race'.[16]

Its writings hold that 'The Word of God' (sacred scriptures) – progressively and successively revealed to humanity by His Prophets – 'is the king of words and its pervasive influence is incalculable. It hath ever dominated and will continue to dominate the realm of being.'[17] Thus the divinely revealed principle of human oneness has 'pervasive influence' for every constructive field of human endeavour, including the field of sports. From this perspective, it is thought that the Games advance what Bahá'í writings hold is the spirit of the present age – the oneness and wholeness of the human race.

The following truth validates the universal, all-embracing character of the standard for all constructive human affairs and proceedings, including sports:

> All the divine Manifestations [Prophets] have proclaimed the oneness of God and the unity of mankind. They have taught that men should love and mutually help each other in order that they might progress. Now if this conception of religion be true, its essential principle is the oneness of humanity. The fundamental truth of the Manifestations is peace. This underlies all religion, all justice. The divine purpose is that men should live in unity, concord and agreement and should love one another. Consider the virtues of the human world and realize that the oneness of humanity is the primary foundation of them all.[18]

Bahá'u'lláh (1817–92), the Prophet-Founder of the Bahá'í Faith, has admirably fulfilled this divine expectation. At the core of this work is the reality that 'the principle of the oneness and wholeness of the human race', is 'the hall-mark of Bahá'u'lláh's Revelation and the pivot of His teachings'. The Bahá'í writings explain:

> Of such cardinal importance is this principle of unity that it is expressly referred to . . . as the central purpose of His Faith . . . the goal that 'excelleth every goal' and an aspiration which is 'the monarch of all aspirations'.[19]

And like all principles, whether called human values or moral or spiritual values, or ethical values, or virtues, such as valour, striving, fairness and teamwork, they induce a 'perspective . . . an attitude, a dynamic, a will, an aspiration, which facilitate the . . . implementation of practical measures'.[20]

Space permits only a few stories which exemplify some of these features. Let's start with two marathon runs.

2
Two Glorious Marathon Runs

According to legend, long ago a Greek herald ran from place to place to secure support for a war and then to the town of Marathon where the battle took place. After Greek soldiers had defeated a foreign army in Marathon, the herald ran 25 miles to Athens to announce the victory, whereupon he collapsed and died.

The first modern Olympic Games held in Athens, Greece, in 1896 extolled the marathon – a long-distance footrace. A crowd of 100,000 people gathered in the stadium to watch it. The Greeks hadn't won a race yet. This was the last race.

A French runner had sprinted to a long lead over the hot and dusty road. When the course went uphill, he slowed down and finally stopped. An Australian then took the lead. But one Greek runner, Spyridon Louis, closed the gap. The crowd shouted 'Hellene! Hellene!', meaning 'A Greek! A Greek!' Louis ran even harder. The Australian fell to the ground. Finally, when Louis entered the stadium, a band followed him on horseback.

Spyridon Louis holding his trophy

The Greek king and queen and thousands of others cheered as he crossed the finish line.[21]

Bahá'u'lláh

Bahá'u'lláh,[22] the Prophet-Founder of the Bahá'í Faith, was exiled from His homeland, Persia (Iran), in 1853, as He was seen as a threat to the leadership of the country. He and His family and other Bahá'ís went to Baghdad where they remained for a decade. Soon Bahá'u'lláh became well known for His wisdom. His enemies had expected Him to be exiled in disgrace but the people of Baghdad poured out their love for Him. The governor admired Him and offered to help in any way he could. People in Baghdad of every sort had been drawn to Bahá'u'lláh. Men of learning and influence were amazed at His vast intuitive knowledge. They were attracted by His luminous character. Nothing dimmed the splendour of His greatness and His loving-kindness.

The Persian government eventually became concerned about the spread of Bahá'u'lláh's influence into Persia and asked the leaders of Baghdad to move Him further from their border. In 1863 He and His family and companions were sent from Baghdad to Constantinople (Istanbul).

Like the Prophets gone before, Bahá'u'lláh made a uniquely penetrating impression on those who encountered Him. His peerless character distinguished Him. The deep spiritual devotion He inspired was due to both His exemplary rectitude of conduct in both His personal and public life, and the powerful influence of His revelation of the Word of God. He upheld that eternal quality of spirit essential to all religions. He sacrificed Himself for the betterment of humanity. He and His designated successors taught that the Golden Rule and the spiritual qualities of love, kindness, courtesy, justice, fairness, patience and detachment were among unnumbered religious virtues all people should manifest. His writings also explain the Creator's displeasure with humanity's disunity.

While Bahá'u'lláh was in Baghdad, on the other side of the

world, America was being torn apart by a civil war over slavery – a grievous practice that Bahá'u'lláh clearly forbade:

> It is forbidden you to trade in slaves, be they men or women. It is not for him who is himself a servant to buy another of God's servants, and this hath been prohibited in His Holy Tablet . . . Let no man exalt himself above another . . .[23]

Bahá'u'lláh's love and His teachings transformed the lives of Bahá'ís in Baghdad. He did everything He could to comfort those who could not accompany Him to Constantinople. He showered them with His love. He wrote to every Bahá'í man, woman, youth and child a parting letter. This inspired them to show forth in their lives their lofty purpose as Bahá'ís by their virtuous deeds.

The Heart of a Champion

Some years before that first modern Olympic marathon in 1896, Mírzá Asadu'lláh, a Bahá'í religious scholar, manifested in 1863 the heart of a champion too. He showed the world he was a part of something much larger and important than himself. Here is what this devoted religious scholar who had left that field to become a humble exile, and who had been forced to remain in Baghdad when Bahá'u'lláh and others departed, said:

> I was so loath to let Him go out of my sight, that I ran after them for three hours.
>
> He saw me, and getting down from His horse, waited for me, telling me with His beautiful voice, full of love and kindness, to go back to Baghdád, and with the friends, to set about our work [teaching the Faith and living its teachings], not slothfully, but with energy:
>
> 'Be not overcome with sorrow – I am leaving friends I love in Baghdád. I will surely send to them tidings of our welfare. Be steadfast in your service to God, who doeth whatsoever He willeth. Live in such peace as will be permitted to you.'

We watched them disappear into the darkness with sinking hearts, for their enemies were powerful and cruel![24]

In 1911 and 1913 'Abdu'l-Bahá, Bahá'u'lláh's eldest son and successor, stayed for some weeks in Paris, visiting the Bahá'í community and giving a number of talks. He urged the Bahá'ís and others to strive to be united by the divine power of an unselfish love which was larger than love of family, love of country.

> When you love a member of your family or a compatriot, let it be with a ray of the Infinite Love! Let it be in God, and for God! Wherever you find the attributes of God love that person, whether he be of your family or of another. Shed the light of a boundless love on every human being whom you meet, whether of your country, your race . . . or of any other nation, colour or shade of political opinion . . .
>
> You will be servants of God, who are dwelling near to Him, His divine helpers in the service, ministering to all Humanity. *All* Humanity! Every human being! *Never forget this!*
>
> Do not say, he is an Italian, or a Frenchman, or an American, or an Englishman, remember only that he is a son of God, a servant of the Most High, a man! All are *men*! Forget nationalities; *all are equal in the sight of God!*[25]

3
Nelson Évora (1984–)

And this commitment to human oneness is exactly what Nelson Évora showed. He hopped, skipped and jumped into history when he won a gold medal in the men's triple jump at the Beijing 2008 Olympics Games.

Évora's family moved from Cape Verde to Outagamie, Ivory Coast, where he was born. When he was five years old they moved to an apartment in the Odivelas region of Lisbon, Portugal. On the floor above lived the former Portugal record-holder in the high jump, João Ganço, and his family. One of his three sons, Davide, was practising athletics. He was just a year older than Nelson and they became best friends.

One day Ganço watched the two boys playing in the street and suggested that Évora start athletics training with him as Nelson's coach. And just like that Évora's athletic career started.

The Évora family and the Ganço family were one, just as Bahá'í teachings say: 'All are [members] of one family, one race; all are human beings.'[26] Évora had an experienced, reliable example to follow. João Ganço taught him the standards, virtues and values needed to striving for excellence, for working hard in tough times. And he had learned religious values in his Bahá'í upbringing. Évora's gold medal proved that in sports – as in every other avenue of life – that following humbly the guidance of one who sets a good example for living, coping and victory is a good teacher. And that 'all virtues have a centre and source. That source is God, from Whom all . . . bounties emanate'.[27]

The motto of the 2008 Games in Beijing was 'One World, One Dream'. The Games likely broadened acceptance of this truth. In the best Olympic tradition, it recognized that there are those who dream for this realization in every field of human endeavour, including sports; hoping and striving in their positive ways that divisive, contrived social differences and erroneous ways of thinking about superiority will eventually be eliminated. The motto reminds us that human oneness is an ancient moral truth.

We'll come to other instances demonstrating that the Bahá'í teachings regarding human oneness do not

> . . . ignore, nor . . . attempt to suppress, the diversity of ethnical origins, of climate, of history, of language and tradition, of thought and habit, that differentiate the peoples and nations of the world. It calls for a wider loyalty, for a larger aspiration . . . Its watchword is 'unity in diversity'. . .[28]

Portugal's Nelson Évora competes in the men's triple jump at the Doha Diamond League

4
Religion and Sports: The Influence of Religious Values

> As religion inculcates morality,
> it is therefore the truest philosophy
> and on it is built the only lasting civilization.[29]

Sports historians have discovered that sport games were created from man's desire to gain, through adherence to religious teachings, victory over foes seen and unseen, to influence the force of nature and to promote fertility among crops and animals.[30]

Peoples in ancient societies rendered homage to family, clan and tribal gods or deities. They invented sport games as a means of advancing unity among themselves. America's oldest team sport, lacrosse, for example, dates back to circa 1100 AD and was developed by Native Americans for community-building purposes. It was played by many indigenous peoples in America and Canada, including the Iroquois, Choctaw, Cherokee and Creek.

The earliest records of the ancient Olympic Games date from 776 BC. According to Paul Christesen, Professor of Ancient Greek History at Dartmouth College, USA, they were a 'religious festival held in a religious sanctuary'.[31] It exalted athletic contests within a religious framework that went back 3,000 years. It honoured the Greek god Zeus, the most important deity in Hellenic society, within a polytheistic culture.[32] Athletic contests expressed the spiritual character of the Games. Following community norms and rituals, contestants took religious oaths and were expected to manifest courage, fortitude, loyalty, excellence, valour, respect and other spiritual qualities.

Baron de Coubertin established the modern Games on the 'indelible' spiritual character of the ancient Olympics. He declared that the Games prevailed because the traditional 'gods' were 'the friends of the Games'.[33] Freedom from religious prejudice has augured well for the Games and the world.

The Bahá'í writings explain that long before the advent of Abraham, Jesus, Muhammad and the other universal Messengers of God, local 'teachers' conveyed to their clans and peoples spiritual and social values and virtues. Since this benevolent divine intervention occurred long ago, before humankind learned to write, most of this grand spiritual and social evolution has been lost to history. 'Abdu'l-Bahá explained:

> . . . there have been many holy Manifestations of God [religious teachers, educators]. One thousand years ago, two hundred thousand years ago, one million years ago the bounty of God [unto mankind] was flowing, the radiance of God was shining, the dominion of God was existing.[34]

Houston Smith in his book *The World's Religions* has written about these ancient religions:

> The written world religions now pretty much cover the world, but chronologically they form only the tip of the religious iceberg; for they span less than four thousand years as compared with the three million years or so of the religions that preceded them. During that immense time span people had what it now largely referred to as primal religions – primal because they came first – sometimes referred to as tribal ['pagan', 'traditional'], because its groupings were small, or oral, because writing was unknown to them. This mode of religiosity continues [for example] in Africa, Australia, Southwest Asia, the Pacific Islands, Siberia [Europe], and among the Indians of North and South America.[35]

Moojan Momen notes:

> ... in surveying the religions of the world, it is necessary to look briefly at the central concepts in primal religions. The wealth of variety of religious manifestation among primal peoples make anything more than a few generalizations about this subject difficult ...
>
> In many primal or tribal religions there are considered to be many spiritual realities, spirits and gods, associated with particular holy places or with important aspects of social life such as the harvest or fertility.[36]

Such was the case with the athletic games in Greece, honouring the male god Zeus. Momen explains that

> As humanity has evolved and become more complex socially, so successive religions have ... [conveyed] an eternal spiritual truth, which is right for all time, social teachings that are appropriate for the time in which the religion appeared.[37]

Thus as centuries passed, people stopped believing in the Greek gods and the games gradually declined, possibly for economic reasons.[38] By 400 AD, after more than a thousand years, the Olympic era was effectively over. But since the ancient Olympic Games were primarily a spiritual affair, some spiritual values naturally transitioned into the modern Games. However, some think that the transition today only 'stages a secular commercialized celebration of a universal humanity'.[39]

5
Of Vision and Action

Born in Paris in 1863, Baron de Coubertin was of a long-established French aristocratic family. Encouraged by the classical idea of balance of mind and body, he actively participated at school in fencing, riding, tennis, boxing and rowing. He rejected careers in the priesthood and diplomacy. An educator, he envisaged for himself a fulfilling role, having 'a higher mission and purpose'. He found direction in encouraging physical education and sports in school systems in France.

While he drew widely on the ideas and experiments of others, he was, as pointed out by David Goldblatt, the first to connect his call for a revival of the Games 'to some form of internationalism'. His social rank and influential personal connections enabled him to promote a universal call. He realized that selfless, sacrificial, effective action was required to achieve the goal of restoring the Games. He tied the revival to the attitudes of 'gentlemen athletes' of his time and created an international social and political coalition, or team, to progress his proposal.[40] 'Perhaps,' Goldblatt suggests, 'Coubertin's greatest advantage was his capacity to think big.'[41] He kept looking at the big picture, the larger purpose, the larger connections. He had his cause, his mentors, his collaborators, and he took action. He ignited 'a serious and sustainable Olympic revival movement'.[42] Coubertin was also the founder of the International Olympic Committee (IOC).

It may be thought that in some ways the modern Olympic Games are a memorial to Pierre Coubertin's lofty vision and noble actions. The 'father' of the modern Olympics brought the world's nations and peoples together under an impressive, appealing Olympic Movement. Its promotion of international cooperation and fellowship is a remarkable development towards human oneness. He saw sports as a higher calling. He was committed to the notion that it could provide vital truths for the modern world. He envisaged that the Games would become both the symbol and centrepiece of a new global era of togetherness among nations and peoples, enhancing moral virtues for the good of humanity.

Still, it may seem remarkable today that the well-educated, well-experienced visionary was inspired by the 'indelibly' religious character of the ancient Olympics. His courage, his acceptance of responsibility, his wise and effective collaborative (or team) actions with prominent and influential persons made the transition to the modern Games happen. He helped them acquire a winning attitude that a sustainable Olympic future was possible.

By 1924, the Games had become more popular than ever. The first radio broadcast of the event occurred that year. Baron de Coubertin had seen the event grow from an idea in 1896 to a popular worldwide celebration. He oversaw his last Olympic Games in Paris in 1924. A founding member of the IOC, he served as its president from 1896 to 1925.

It easy to imagine Coubertin's heart swollen with joy as he introduced the French President who officially declared the Paris Olympic Games 1924 open to a crowd of about sixty thousand in the Combes Stadium on Saturday 5 July 1924. Forty-five nations competed. He had been instrumental in expanding thinking about sports in general and especially about the need for the modern Olympic Games.

It is not surprising that the role and power of vision influenced the Paris 2024 Games. Campaigning for her city to host the Games after a terrorist attack in 2015, Mayor Anne Hidalgo explained in an interview:

> We need to do something that is unifying. Something that is very powerful, very peaceful and allows us to move forward. So, I threw myself into it.[43]

Which calls to mind this thought from the Bahá'í teachings:

> . . . the promotion of the oneness of the kingdom of humanity . . . is the essence of the teachings of all the Manifestations [Prophets] of God . . .[44]

As stated earlier, a springboard for considering the possible application of the major principle of the Bahá'í Faith to the Olympics is its capacity to induce vision and action. 'Abdu'l-Bahá said in Paris,

> What profit is there in . . . talking of the solidarity of the human race as a grand ideal? Unless these thoughts are translated into the world of action, they are useless.
> The wrongs in the world continue to exist just because people talk only of their ideals, and do not strive to put them into practice.[45]

> Do not allow difference of opinion, or diversity of thought to separate you from your fellow-men, or to be the cause of dispute, hatred and strife in your hearts.
> Rather search diligently for the truth and make all men your friends.[46]

6
The Victory of the Covenant

> The divine prophets . . . have laid down certain laws and
> heavenly principles for the guidance of mankind.
> They have . . . established praiseworthy ethical ideals
> and inculcated the highest standards of virtue in the human
> world.[47]

God has sent to humanity universal Prophets, Whose teachings and deeds have progressively and successively fostered mankind's spiritual and social development – Abraham, Krishna, Zoroaster, Buddha, Moses, Jesus, Muhammad, the Báb (1819–50) and now Bahá'u'lláh (1817–92). The Báb heralded Bahá'u'lláh's advent.

Bahá'u'lláh is the Prophet-Founder of the Bahá'í Faith, which was established in Iran in the mid-1800s. He taught that all the world's major religions are based on sacred scriptures provided one God and that all people are dependent upon God.

> History has shown that 'the divine religions . . . lead their
> true followers to sincerity of intent, to high purpose . . . to
> the keeping of their covenants . . . to concerns for the rights
> of others . . . to justice in every aspect of life . . . and to
> unflagging efforts in the service of mankind.[48]

Bahá'u'lláh suffered persecution because of His new teachings on the oneness of religion and the oneness of all peoples. Over 20,000 early followers were killed. He was imprisoned, tortured and exiled from Iran to various places within the Ottoman Empire. In 1868 He was sent as a prisoner to the fortress city of 'Akká in the Holy Land in the vicinity of the hamlet where He passed away in 1892.

Baháʼís recognize that an important way in which the creative power of the revelation of God's guidance works its influence on the human world is through progressive movements that are 'akin to various Baháʼí principles'. Over 80 years ago it was noted that 'the principles of Baháʼu'lláh have been adopted by thinking people all over this planet'.⁴⁹ In 1896, for example, just 33 years after Baháʼu'lláh began His prophetic mission for the unification and transformation of society to a global civilization, the first modern international Olympic Games were held in Athens.

Before His passing, Baháʼu'lláh appointed His eldest son, ʻAbduʼl-Bahá (1844–1921) to succeed Him in guiding the Baháʼí world community. He urged believers to follow His son's behaviour and ways of serving humanity.

ʻAbduʼl-Bahá's Sports Activities

Like his Father, ʻAbduʼl-Bahá demonstrated signs of excellence in His sporting activities. He enjoyed horse riding and was 'a fearless horseman'.⁵⁰ He was also 'a strong and graceful swimmer'.⁵¹

ʻAbduʼl-Bahá in turn appointed His eldest grandson, Shoghi Effendi (1897–1957) as His successor. He urged Baháʼís to remember ʻAbduʼl-Bahá's 'courage, His genuine love', 'those unforgettable and historic episodes and occasions on which He so strikingly demonstrated His keen sense of justice, His spontaneous sympathy for the downtrodden, His ever-abiding sense of the oneness of the human race, His overflowing love for its members . . .'⁵²

Shoghi Effendi Excelled in Sports

In his insightful essay 'Function of Sports in Life', written when he was a full-time university student at the American University of Beirut in 1915, Shoghi Effendi noted:

> Sports have existed in the past ages and have played an important role in the history of mankind . . . The ancient

Greeks deeply felt the indispensability of sports, they stuck to it and it is out of these marvellous Olympian games that Sparta got such renown and reputation . . .

In America and England people were so convinced of the noble function of sports in life that they started to revive the old Olympian Games . . . The Romans admired the success of the Greek athletic life and . . . in 186 B.C. professional Greek sportsmen established a series of sports in Rome . . . it is sufficient to say the influence which these sports exerted upon the Roman citizens cannot be estimated . . .

. . . athletics, a branch of sports, is of great advantage to life. Athletics are necessary if not indispensable for the future success of the nation as well as of the individual. 'A sound mind in a sound body' was the motto of the Greeks and the model of the strong, healthy and vigorous Spartans. Their carrying out of the plan was a cause for the long existence of Greece and for its luxuriant literary culture . . .

Athletics refresh the body, tranquillize and enlighten the mind, and develop moral character . . .

Sports, in general, have had an important and estimable function in life and will inevitably in future be regarded as the indispensable factor for intellectual and moral growth.[53]

Regarding his observation that 'Athletics . . . develop moral character,' Shoghi Effendi, later, in his position as the international head of the Bahá'í Faith, shared Bahá'u'lláh's words:

The light of a good character surpasseth the light of the sun and the radiance thereof. Whoso attaineth unto it is accounted as a jewel among men. The glory and upliftment of the world must needs depend upon it.[54]

The purpose of the one true God in manifesting Himself . . . is to array every man with the mantle of a saintly character, and to adorn him with the ornament of holy and good deeds.[55]

When he was a student at Oxford University, Shoghi Effendi loved tennis, a game in which he excelled. His speed in hitting the ball and his enjoyment of the game was greatly admired. One of his English tennis partners remarked:

> I used to play tennis with him in the Master's Field and marvellously active he was . . . He was ambidextrous and switched his racket from one hand to the other for a volley or the net with lightning speed – but not in a grimly earnest manner. On the contrary, he was laughing . . . most of the time.[56]

Another student remarked:

> An example of his intrepid spirit. I remember hearing of him that he had addressed Hopkins, an American Rhodes Scholar with the words: 'Hopkins! I hear that you are Tennis Blue [the highest honour granted to an individual sportsperson at the University of Oxford]. Let's have a game sometime.'[57]

During the 'walk' or 'climb' excursions, over the mountain passes at Interlaken, Switzerland, Shoghi Effendi sometimes took after he became the head of the Faith in 1921, he often walked 10 to 16 hours, usually alone. He climbed high mountain peaks, roped to a guide, with 'indefatigable energy and determination'. His longest walk was 42 kilometres over two passes.[58]

The Universal House of Justice, the internationally elected governing body of the worldwide Bahá'í community since 1963, provides guidance relevant to every field of constructive human endeavours, including the world of sports. In its letter to the President of Brazil on the occasion of its hosting the World Cup Games in 2014, it observed that the Games were held within 'the global culture', 'a global civilization', that has 'emerged in this age', 'as the world advances in its organic evolution'. It described it as an 'extraordinary footballing spectacle'.

Shoghi Effendi (wearing goggles) with a party of climbers and their guides in the Swiss Alps

Moreover, it set out certain 'qualities' shown during the world tournament that 'inspire observers' to manifest them 'in their lives'.

It wrote that the World Cup tournament and its observers were 'strengthened by the marvellous diversity of the participants'; that 'to rejoice in this fact is to reject prejudice in all its forms'; and that 'summoning together the nations in friendship, powerfully suggests that collaboration and common endeavour are possible in all things'. The House of Justice, reflecting on the 'many qualities' of the Brazilian people, noted that 'the path to peace' will require

> . . . expansive hearts, a passion for progress, unbounded creative energy, great resilience, a strength forged from diversity, and minds enlightened by the spirit of the age and inspired by the quest for justice. The peoples of the world are as variegated flowers in one splendid garden.

> ... A sporting contest, even one on such a scale as this, cannot obscure the severity of the challenges that confront humankind. But in the weeks to come, we hope that observers everywhere – especially the youth of the world – will take heart from the many examples of teamwork, fair play, valour, and earnest striving that are sure to surface in the tournament [and] they will aspire to show those same qualities in their lives, in service to their communities, and in the promotion of peace.[59]

It is easy to understand that all the clarifications included in the House of Justice's letter of 2014 are, of course, applicable to the 'extraordinary' Olympic Games. Along this line, David Goldblatt has emphasized in his book *The Games: A Global History of the Olympics* there is in the modern Games 'a celebration of sport's capacity to level social differences, to make talent and ability transparent in an otherwise unjust world'.[60]

The Universal House of Justice also indicated in its letter of October 1985 to the Peoples of the World[61] regarding the promise of global peace, some implications of the principle of the oneness of humanity and its application to 'all fields of human endeavour':

> Racism, one of the most baleful and persistent evils, is a major barrier to peace. Its practice perpetuates too outrageous a violation of the dignity of human beings to be countenanced under any pretext. Racism retards the unfoldment of the boundless potentialities of its victims, corrupts its perpetrators, and blights human progress. Recognition of the oneness of mankind, implemented by appropriate legal measures, must be universally upheld if this problem is to be overcome.

Regarding the equality of men and women, it wrote:

> The emancipation of women, the achievement of full equality between the sexes, is one of the most important,

though less acknowledged prerequisites of peace. The denial of such equality perpetrates an injustice against one half of the world's population and promotes in men harmful attitudes and habits that are carried from the family to the workplace, to political life, and ultimately to international relations. There are no grounds, moral, practical, or biological, upon which such denial can be justified. Only as women are welcomed into full partnership in all fields of human endeavour will the moral and psychological climate be created in which international peace can emerge.

It emphasized that the 'universal acceptance' of the 'spiritual principle' of human oneness 'is essential to any successful attempt to establish world peace. It should therefore be universally proclaimed, taught in schools, and constantly asserted in every nation as preparation for the organic change in . . . society which it implies.'[62]

H.C. Baldry wrote in his work *The Unity of Mankind in Greek Thought* that Socrates, the great Greek philosopher, had a 'profound influence on Greek ideas about the unity and the division of the human race', advanced new ways of thinking that lifted people above the prejudices of the day and held that 'true wisdom' was influenced by inner character and right actions.[63]

According to Baldry, 'Socrates observed that there were three types of people who attended Olympic Games: "those who came to buy and sell, those who come to compete, and those who come to look on". He thought "the best of them" were those who "opened their hearts and minds to the edifying purpose and influence of the Games". The relationship between those open to new learning . . . was a crucial issue in Greek thought regarding "the nature of human society, the unity of mankind, and the Olympic Games".'[64]

7
Striving 'Together' with Religious Values

> All things must have a cause, a motive power,
> an animating principle.[65]

The original Olympic motto adopted in 1894 was 'Faster – Higher – Stronger'. However in 2021 the International Olympic Committee (IOC) approved a change. The new motto is 'Faster, Higher, Stronger – Together'.[66] The IOC feels it 'recognizes the unifying power of sports and the importance of solidarity'.[67] IOC President Thomas Bach has asserted, 'When we do sport, it inspires us to always give it our best, and it makes us dream, it spreads joy and brings us together.'[68]

The 'Together' theme affirms that the intent of the Olympic Games is to advance symbolically the oneness of humanity. It affirms as well that the true star of the Olympics has been its victorious 'together[ness]' or teamwork virtue or quality. Athletes, coaches, trainers, fans, spectators, Olympic officials, governments, public and private international, national and local groups have worked heroically together as one, in the service to humanity that the Olympics have provided. As indicated above, 'excellence, respect and friendship' are core values upon which the Olympic movement 'builds its activities to promote sport, culture and education with a view to building a better world'.[69] Below are extracts from Bahá'í writings which illustrate the importance of these 'unifying' virtues.

> All the Manifestations of God came with the same purpose, and they have all sought to lead men into the paths of virtue.[70]

Excellence

> ... man's distinction lieth in the excellence of his conduct and in the pursuit of that which beseemeth his station.[71]

> In everything we do we should always try to attain a standard of excellence.[72]

> So high must be your standard of excellence ... that the moral influence you exert penetrates the consciousness of the wider community.[73]

Friendship

> So free must your thoughts and action be of any trace of prejudice – racial, religious, economic, national, tribal, class, or cultural – that even the stranger sees in you loving friends.[74]

> What profit is there in agreeing that universal friendship is good, and talking of the solidarity of the human race as a grand ideal. Unless these thoughts are translated into the world of action, they are useless.[75]

> Do not be content in showing friendship in words alone, let your heart burn with loving kindness for all who may cross your path.[76]

The Universal House of Justice has asked:

> Where else but in Bahá'u'lláh's principle of the oneness of humankind can the world find a vision broad enough to unite all its diverse elements? How else but by translating that vision into an order based on unity in diversity can the world heal the social fractures that divide it? ... Extend then to everyone the hand of friendship, of common endeavour, of shared service, of collective learning, and advance as one.[77]

Numerous instances of true friendship have been an endearing feature of the Games. In a qualifying round for the long jump at the Berlin Olympics in 1936 Jesse Owens, a black American, took a practice walk into the long-jump pit. Although he hadn't jumped, officials counted his walk into the pit as his first try. Some German officials openly showed their hostility towards black contestants. They believed they were inferior. Hitler and the Nazis politicized and nationalized the Olympics as never before. They viewed the Games as a means to spread their false doctrine of Aryan superiority, racial hatred and nationalistic ideology. They began the practice of adding up the medals each country's athletes won. It was the first country to claim it 'won' the Olympics.

Jesse Owens was very upset. Suddenly, the German jumper Luz Long came over. He gave Owens a tip for the jump. Owens listened. And he went on to win gold. Long warmly congratulated him. The black athlete and the white German athlete became friends. They walked together around the stadium. Owens said his friendship with Long was more important than any of the Olympic medals he won. Hitler refused to congratulate him.[78]

Respect

In the Barcelona Olympics 1992, a South African team competed in the Olympics for the first time in 36 years. Elana Meyer, who was white, was its runner in the women's 10,000 metre race. Derartu Tulu was a black runner from Ethiopia. The two runners led the pack. Finally, Tulu pulled ahead to finish first. She was the first black African woman to win a gold medal. Meyer hugged her. Then Tulu grabbed Meyer's hand. Together they started the victory lap around the stadium. It was a historic symbolic image of human oneness. 'It captured the Olympic spirit.'[79]

8

'The greatest bestowal of God to man is the capacity to attain human virtues.'[80]

In its letter written on the occasion of the World Cup in 2014, the Universal House of Justice shared this hopeful vision of the future:

> We anticipate a time when competition among the nations may be a phenomenon chiefly witnessed in the sporting arena, whereas interactions on the global stage will be dominated by cooperation, reciprocity, and mutual support. We pray that this present occasion . . . will inspire not only passing fellowship but lasting solidarity among all who participate and the countless millions who spectate.[81]

As stated above, the House of Justice identified other spiritual qualities which should be demonstrated in and outside of sports and which Olympians should manifest:

Fairness

> . . . we hope that observers everywhere – especially the youth of the world – will take heart from the many examples of . . . fair play . . . that are sure to surface in the tournament. God willing, they will aspire to show those same qualities in their lives, in service to their communities, and in the promotion of peace.[82]

Striving

... we hope that observers everywhere – especially the youth of the world – will take heart from the many examples of ... earnest striving ... that are sure to surface in the tournament. God willing, they will aspire to show those same qualities in their lives, in service to their communities, and in the promotion of peace.[83]

Bahá'u'lláh has drawn the circle of unity, He has made a design for the uniting of all the peoples, and for the gathering of them all under the shelter of the tent of universal unity ... we must all strive with heart and soul until we have the reality of unity in our midst, and as we work, so will strength be given unto us. Leave all thought of self, and strive only to be obedient and submissive to the Will of God.[84]

Valour

... we hope that observers everywhere – especially the youth of the world – will take heart from the many examples of ... valour ... that are sure to surface in the tournament. God willing, they will aspire to show those same qualities in their lives, in service to their communities, and in the promotion of peace.[85]

Teamwork

... we hope that observers everywhere – especially the youth of the world – will take heart from the many examples of ... teamwork ... that are sure to surface in the tournament. God willing, they will aspire to show those same qualities in their lives, in service to their communities, and in the promotion of peace.[86]

... recognize the benefit that accrues from the contribution of each individual to the progress of the whole, and thus the service rendered by each one, in keeping with the possibilities created by a person's circumstances, [should be] welcomed by all.'[87]

Whether labouring for the elimination of every trace of racism and discrimination, championing the equality of women and men, or seeking to advance justice, the efforts of every member of the human family are necessary. Constructive change is possible everywhere. Man, woman, youth, and child – all have an essential contribution to make.[88]

9
A Team Victory

> . . . we must endeavour through the assistance and grace of
> God . . . to attain all lofty virtues,
> that we may witness the effulgence of the Sun of Reality,
> reflect the spirit of the Kingdom . . .
> live in conscious at-one-ment with the eternal world
> and become quickened
> and awake with the life and love of God.[89]

Important features regarding the spiritual qualities of teamwork for the unification of humankind were demonstrated in 1849 by Bábís, under Bahá'u'lláh's direction, at the shrine of Shaykh Ṭabarsí, Persia. He also showed how spiritual victories should be measured.

Bábís were viciously attacked by local religious leaders and their followers. Seeking a place of safety, they took refuge in the small shrine and constructed walls around to create a fortress. Bahá'u'lláh in His home at Tehran heard of this and He decided to visit the hastily constructed fort.

His visit instilled an exuberant spirit of joy and courage in every heart. He gave spiritual and practical directions. They enabled everyone to work better together. He inspected the fort and was satisfied with work that had been accomplished to improve conditions inside and outside the building.[90] After His visit a moat was dug around the fort as a safeguard against attack.[91]

Bahá'u'lláh told his brave companions: 'You have been chosen of God to be . . . the establishers of His Faith . . . Whatever may befall, victory is yours, a victory which is complete and certain.'[92]

Being with Bahá'u'lláh, moved by His words, the defenders came to appreciate more fully that their Faith called for a 'wider loyalty', for a 'larger aspiration'[93] than they had before. And this awareness among believers that a 'broader', 'larger', 'wider' consciousness of the sacred aim and purpose of their Faith animates Bahá'í individuals and groups, and teams up to today.

Bahá'u'lláh's promise He would soon return to the believers from His home in Tehran greatly strengthened them. However, on His way back to Ṭabarsí with provisions and with more Bábís, He was arrested by enemies. He was strictly imprisoned and severely tortured. After some time, He was sent back to Tehran.[94] Remembering His guidance on staying united, working together, the innocent defenders endured a horrible siege. It lasted 11 months. Still, at their leader's command, 'Mount your steeds, O Heroes of God,'[95] they sallied out the fort as one team over and over again, defending their faith. Each time they swept the enemy aside.

Because no food or water could be brought into the fort, the time came when they ate grass, the leaves of trees, and the boiled leather of saddles. At one time, they went 18 days with no food at all but the leather of their shoes. Still, their faith that God would render His Cause victorious sustained them. When the army prepared to mount a massive attack, it looked like the believers weakened by thirst and hunger would be defeated. Then, unexpectedly it rained and rained many days. Then it snowed. The soldiers couldn't walk or ride their horses or move their cannons and other weapons across the cold, wet, muddy grounds. At last water was available. Food was snuck into the fort.

Finally, the spirit of the army of 12,000 government soldiers broke. The courageous defenders had withstood every attack. They had remained united, one virtuous team, invigorated throughout by a shared vision and purpose. They had supported one another as best they could. They had loved one another. They had lived and survived without complaining of sufferings and hardships. No one had criticized another, or had engaged in backbiting or gossip. No one had thought he was superior. Their faith, their vision, their dreams and hopes of making a difference in the world were stronger and larger, and broader than their individual selves, and all other considerations.

Realizing that his well-armed army was defeated by an untrained, inexperienced team of humble individuals who'd risked their lives for the noble vision they had embraced, the field commander swore this on a Qur'án: if the Bábís ceased fighting and came outside they would not be harmed. Once they did, the sworn oath was forgotten. Most of the defenceless believers were pitilessly struck down in a frenzy of hate. But survivors went on to tell the world, in their own ways, that the little band of faithful redeemers had achieved that 'complete and certain victory' Bahá'u'lláh had promised. They had shown that God was always the Victorious.

Perhaps, they were among those whom Bahá'u'lláh remembered when He later revealed: 'If these companions be not the true strivers after God, who else could be called by this name.'[96]

The prevailing spiritual darkness in some circles even today suggests it might be imagined that the Olympic flame itself might glow in Games to come more nobly, as Bahá'u'lláh notes: 'The Word of God hath set the heart of the world afire . . .'[97] It is easy to imagine, as well, that in the days to come humanity might wonder how authorities up in the mountains of Mákú denied the Báb even a candle to light His prison cell. 'Abdu'l-Bahá envisioned 'a day . . . in which the oneness of humankind shall uplift its standard and . . . like the true morning, flood the world with its light'.[98]

Heart

The manner in which the victors at Ṭabarsí served human oneness may give some insights into what it means to show 'heart' when facing staggering challenges. Among athletes, and many others, it is regarded as an essential value.[99] The Bábís and early Bahá'ís showed it on a grand scale. And no one better than 'Abdu'l-Bahá!

All the world loves persons involved in wholesome contests who refuse to give in, who do not accept defeat when it seems reasonable to do so. It might be thought an irrational commitment to an enterprise. It might be considered a naïve, innocent commitment to a 'strange' force or movement. A lack of self-concern. One may recall the ruthless slanders and persecutions inflicted upon the early disciples of Abraham, Moses, Jesus, Muhammad, Buddha and upon early disciples of other universal Prophets. History shows that they resolutely gave themselves over to new divine callings when others feared to consider them or were indifferent. They came to understand, as did the Bábís at Ṭabarsí, that true spiritual victories are first experienced in the heart.[100]

Once when some of the impoverished Ṭabarsí defenders, undaunted by the seemingly invincible forces arrayed against them, had penetrated a section of the army's encampment which had been occupied by a prince of royal blood, who had narrowly escaped the invasion, they found coffers filled with gold and silver. They disdained to touch any piece of the treasures. 'With the exception of a pot of gunpowder and a favourite sword of the prince which they took as an evidence of their triumph', and which they gave to their leader, Mullá Ḥusayn, they ignored everything else.[101]

* * *

It is not surprising that the ancient virtue of teamwork has been witnessed in many Bahá'í and Olympics experiences. Notwithstanding the popularity of that standard today in many circles, it is often proclaimed to be a unique secular notion without any spiritual foundation. This seems an encouraging development for learning and respecting different approaches.

From his Christian faith, his biblical studies, which greatly influenced his professional career as an outstanding football team player, a professional football team coach, who coached a team that won the American football 'Superbowl', and from his experience as a highly admired consultant to professional football teams and other organizations on teamwork, Tony Dungy offers in his book *The Soul of a Team* some spiritual 'principles which he feels apply to all teams, whether within a family unit, a company or church, or a high school drama club'. He adopted the view that 'these principles will hold true for any business, non-profit, church, or other type of organization. The key is getting everyone on your team to commit.'

He created the acronym 'SOUL'. Each letter describes a feature of teamwork. The framework he adopted is based on the following four principles, which, he makes clear, 'are actually rooted in Scripture'.

The letter S stands for 'Selflessness': 'Putting individual needs aside for the good of the team.' He has observed 'that [this principle] often conflicts with a natural desire for self-advancement'. But, 'Truly selfless team members are not only confident of their own abilities, but use them as 'gifts' that can be used to help others.' He cites the apostle Paul: 'Be humble... Don't look out only for your own interests, but take an interest in others, too' (Philippians 2:34). Dungy emphasizes 'Others have dreams and passions too. The people who hold them are important too [as members of the team].'

O –'Ownership':'Fulfiling your [team] role by learning it thoroughly and by consistently given 100 percent.'

U – 'Unity': 'Understanding and rallying around your team's mission, philosophy, and culture through open communication and positive conflict resolution.' He emphasizes that 'a team that isn't unified and headed in the same direction isn't much of a team at all. It's simply a collection of individuals.' Dungy offers this suggestion which the apostle Peter gave to a group of early Christians facing signs of intense disunity: 'All of you should be of one mind. Sympathize with each other. Love each other as brothers and sisters. Be tenderhearted and keep a humble attitude' (1 Peter 3:8).

L – 'Larger Purpose': 'Contributing to the wider community in a lasting and significant way.' He found that it ' imbues meaning into everything a team member does. It captures the imagination of team members no matter their roles or positions within the organization. It leads to tangible acts and relationships that create opportunities and offers hope to others.'[102]

What seems important is that people around the world are adopting what they feel are true, excellent and reliable frameworks for thinking and acting in ways that cultivate, nourish and strengthen human relationships, no matter how an approach is metaphorically described or framed. The Bahá'í writings suggest that in all circumstances there are 'spiritual prerequisites', 'preeminent and vital', 'basic requirements',[103] and 'a high standard of moral conduct'[104] that govern all Bahá'í activities. These requirements are 'a high sense of moral rectitude'[integrity], 'absolute chastity' and complete 'freedom from [all forms of] prejudice'.[105] These 'prerequisites' interrelate, of course, with what has been set out above about serving human oneness in every situation with a 'larger, wider, broader' consciousness.

The Universal House of Justice has urged Bahá'ís

> . . . to exemplify rectitude of conduct in every aspect of their lives – in their business dealings, in their domestic lives, in all manner of employment, in every service they render to the Cause and to their people – and to observe its requirements in their uncompromising adherence to the laws and principles of the Faith.[106]

Striving

> Strive diligently to acquire virtues befitting your degree and station.[107]

> It is incumbent upon every man of insight and understanding to strive to translate that which hath been written into reality and action . . . That one indeed is a man who, today, dedicateth himself to the service of the entire human race . . . Blessed and happy is he that ariseth to promote the best interests of the peoples and kindreds of the earth . . .[108]

10
Catherine 'Cathy' Freeman (1973–)

The indigenous Australian sprinter Catherine Astrid Salome Freeman specialized in the 400 metres event. Born in 1973 at Slade Point, Mackay, Queensland, she was successful in athletics events at school and, when she was only 16 years old, became the first indigenous Australian to win a goal medal in the 1990 Commonwealth games. Four years later, in the 1994 Commonwealth Games, she won gold medals in both the 200 metre and the 400 metre races. In 1996 Olympics she won a silver medal.

She lit the Olympic flame during the opening ceremony of the 2000 summer Olympics held in Australia before a hundred thousand cheering fans. She was the first indigenous Australian to take part in an opening ceremony in this way.

Freeman's people have lived in Australia for thousands of years, long before Europeans arrived, but they were treated by them as inferior people. Freeman was in some ways a symbol of Australian unity. The whole world rooted for her. The pressure on her to win her race was intense. She took in the audience's emotion and turned it into strength. She came out at the start of her race in third place and crossed the finish line first, becoming the Olympic champion for the women's 400 metres and the second indigenous Australian Olympic gold medallist. Overwhelmed, she sat on the ground for a moment. When she took her victory lap, she held two flags: the Australian and the Aborigine.

Since retiring from athletics in 2003, Freeman has been involved in a number of community and charitable activities, including an Ambassador of the Australian Indigenous Education Foundation. In 2007 she founded the Cathy

CATHERINE 'CATHY' FREEMAN (1973–)

Freeman Foundation, now known as Murrup, an Aboriginal Community Controlled Organisation supporting First Nations children, young people and their families in four remote communities with programmes enabling them to thrive in school and into the future.

Freeman's mother raised her children as Catholics, becoming a Baháʼí in her later years.[109] Freemen herself has described how she was raised as a Baháʼí and was influenced by it,[110] saying of her faith, 'I like the prayers and I appreciate their values about the equality of all human kind.'[111]

11
Edward P. Hurt (1900–89)

Increasingly, over the years, athletes from a diversity of racial and ethnic backgrounds competed in the Games. But it took some time before a little diversity was achieved in the IOC or on National Olympic Committees. This bothered Edward Hurt. A tremendously successful black coach at Morgan State University, a small black university in Baltimore, Maryland, he persevered in his striving for change until he himself was selected in 1960 to the US Olympic Committee. With his impeccable character, moral courage, his straightforward and unassuming manner, his keen insights concerning the broad area of athletics, he dedicated himself to the principles of the Olympics and advanced its goals.

In 1964 he was appointed national Olympic Track and Field Coach for the Japan Olympics 1964. Hurt tackled the task with his customary vigour. His accomplishments were outstanding. His team performed far above expectation.

Hurt held fast to his moral conviction:

> No matter what you're doing, you have to dream. You set goals and you try to reach them. I haven't done nearly all I've wanted to do or dreamed of doing . . . If I have done anything at all, it's because of the other coaches, the men, the college, the administration, alumni, friends, and just everybody. I've only had one formula, and that's hard work.[112]

In his 'true humility', he knew he needed assistance from God, his family, friends, colleagues, traditions, institutions and from moral values. They supported and inspired him along the way.

EDWARD P. HURT (1900–89)

He never considered the honours he gained as personal accomplishments. His favourite response to praise was: 'Heaven is my home, but I ain't homesick.'[113] In other words, it likely meant he had a lofty vision, grounded on spiritual or heavenly values, but virtuous action was required in this world towards achieving it.

Hurt was selected an All-American football player when he was a student at Howard University. From 1932 to 1939 his football teams at Morgan State won 54 games without defeat. George Rhoden was his 400 metre winner in the 1952 Helsinki Games. Josh Culbreath won a bronze medal in the 400 metre hurdles in the 1956 Australia Games. He won 14 championships within Morgan's athletic association. Two of his players, Len Ford and Rosey Brown, were inducted into the American Professional Football Hall of Fame. He won many local and national honours for overall achievements, particularly in the field of coaching and winning championship medals at the national Penn Relays track and field meets.

Among his achievements were US coaching staff for the Pan American Games 1959; United States Olympic Committee Award for Service to the Olympics, 1964; US Olympic Track and Field Games Committee, 1960–72; elected to the National Track and Field Hall of Fame of the United States of America, 1975: elected Helms Foundation Hall of Fame (track coaches) 1953; One of the Outstanding Football Coaches of all Times, University of Texas, 1950; listed among football coaches of the year 1959 by members of the Coaches Association of America and Associated Press.

His devotion to his profession enabled black athletes to demonstrate their talents in venues that had been closed to them before. The back cover of a book written about him notes:

> The arrival of the black athlete on the national sports scene in the 1940s and 50s goes directly back to Edward P. Hurt. There is not a single black sports figure in the world today who is not in some small way in the debt of Coach Hurt.

And to the extent that Hurt helped to break down racial barriers, our entire country owes him a huge debt of gratitude. We are a better nation because of him.[114]

Once, when one of his runners had settled into a slower pace in the back stretch of the quarter mile race, Hurt yelled, 'Run from there!' The runner was startled. He burst into an all-out sprint until he hit the tape. It became a Morgan battle cry. It meant 'Give it all you've got no matter what the situation.' Hurt had that quality known as 'heart', that of pulling up values deep within oneself when facing challenges.

12
Matthew Bullock (1881–1972): Serving Human Oneness

> The lovers of mankind, these are the superior men,
> of whatever nation, creed, or colour they may be.[115]

Edward Hurt was preceded by Matthew Bullock. He was one of those early nationally successful African American athletes, coaches and administrators of sports activities. Among the most successful athletes of his time, he showed how vision, action and faith could change situations. He too has left an enduring example of how sports can instil values, virtues and qualities that build character.

He was born in Dabney, North Carolina, to Jesse and Amanda Bullock, both of whom had been born slaves. They moved in 1889 to the Boston area with seven children and ten dollars. Matthew became a star athlete in high school. He was the first African American captain of any white high school team, captain of the hockey, baseball and football teams. He saw things in a larger way for action, so he could overcome moments of disappointment, failure and heartbreak.

He helped his white teammates realize that they had a common purpose they could rally around. He enrolled at Dartmouth College in 1901. He was the first and only black athlete at Dartmouth on its football and the track teams for four years. He graduated in 1904 with scholastic and athletic distinctions. He graduated from Harvard Law School (1904–7). He paid his tuition by coaching football at a white high school and at a college. He was the first black football coach of an integrated college team and at a local high school. In 1908

Matthew Bullock

Bullock accepted a position as football coach, athletic director and lecturer at Morehouse College. He worked as Dean at another college and as a lawyer in Atlanta, winning distinction for his professional and community services.

Bullock became a member of the Bahá'í Faith in 1940. He often spoke of the pleasure he had in reading Bahá'í teachings.[116]

Over many years he was able to connect his professional and community experiences with religious activities. He spoke at meetings extensively at home and abroad on the Bahá'í principle of the oneness of humanity. In 1970 he was awarded an honorary degree from Harvard University. This was followed by Dartmouth in 1971, with an honorary degree in law. He was accorded a standing ovation among the 5,000 present in honour of his services to human oneness throughout his youth and adult life. The citation read in part:

> Concern for your fellow man continued to occupy your energies after retirement. You are a recognized leader of the Bahá'í Faith, and you have travelled all over the world at your own expense in the interest of that religion. You believe very deeply that the establishment of universal justice and freedom requires the spiritual and moral awakening of all people.[117]

13

Unity in Freedom

Coubertin crossed the executive finishing line as an IOC member with honour. He had contributed much by 1924 towards making the revival of the Olympic Games an extraordinary achievement. As Goldblatt points out, under the circumstances of his time, 'It was not quite Coubertin's intention to create a global stage on which battles for equality and inclusion along the lines of class, ethnicity, gender, disability and sexuality might be fought out.'[118] He kept in mind opportunities and limitations.

He was no doubt thrilled by those 45 national flags fluttering in freedom and promise over the occasion. And speaking of freedom, one of those 'candles of unity' (directions for establishing unity among nations and peoples found in the Bahá'í writings) is 'unity in freedom'.[119] After World War I and World War II many athletes at Olympics Games were from countries which had recently been freed from colonial domination. Many new national flags had been designed and first flown with wet eyes, high heads, shoulders thrown back, hearts beating fast with a gladness words couldn't express. They symbolized that people in the country were living once again in lands of the free.

Interestingly enough in 1956, John Wing, an Australian student, suggested to the IOC that all athletes from all the different countries march as one team during the closing ceremony. They did. This 'together' march became 'another Olympic tradition'.[120] It could be said that those flags 'together' symbolize humanity's longing for freedom from disunity. Perhaps they were a sign that the tide of history was hastening that day when all the peoples of the world would regard 'every foreign land . . .

a fatherland';[121] 'regard themselves as citizens of one common fatherland';[122] dwelling 'in one common fatherland, which is the planet itself'.[123]

14
Harold Abrahams's (1899–1978) Race: A Run Beyond Class and Religion

'Do your best. That's all we can expect.'
The Prince of Wales to Harold Abrahams

The spectacular races run in the 1924 Paris Olympics by the English runner Harold Abrahams and the Scottish runner Eric Liddell are remembered. Their unshakable religious convictions, their extraordinary athletic prowess honoured those Games. Both found there the fulfilment of their highest dreams.

Harold Abrahams was born in Bedford in 1899 to Jewish parents. His father had emigrated to England from Polish Lithuania, then part of the Russian Empire. He attended two fee-paying schools, Bedford School and then Repton School in Derbyshire, where he was a victim of anti-Semitism and felt bullied and alone.[124] He began running as a youth.

Abrahams continued to compete as a runner while at Cambridge. Although he was given a place in the British team for the 1920 Olympics, he was eliminated in the quarter-finals of both the 100 metre and the 200 metre, and finished 20th in the long jump. He was also part of the British team that took fourth place in the 4 × 100 metre relay. However, he never stopped trying to improve his athletic skills.

After he left Cambridge, he engaged a professional coach of Syrian, Italian and French descent, Scipio Africanus 'Sam' Mussabini. His coaching enabled Abrahams to improve significantly. Both Abrahams and Liddell were accepted to represent

Harold Abrahams, Paris 1924

Great Britain in the 1924 Olympics in Paris. They raced against each other only twice, first in a heat of the 200 metres in the 1923 AAA Championship at Stamford Bridge, which Liddell won, and second in the 200 metre final at the 1924 Olympics, where Liddell came in third and Abrahams sixth.

Because Liddell's religious convictions prevented him from racing on a Sunday, when a heat for the 100 metre race was to be held, he could not qualify for the final. Although the 100 metre was his best event, he applied for the 200 metre and 400 metre races instead. This left his teammate Harold Abrahams running in the 100 metre final on 7 July without having to compete against his sporting rival, who was widely thought to be the only British runner able to beat the Americans, who 'had come to look upon the 100 metres race as their own',[125] making Liddell's absence deeply regretted by much of the British public.

The final of the 100 meters was a great event, the fastest race, with several world-famous athletes racing against each other. The track officials showed the six runners to their lanes. The starter's pistol launched the runners. Abrahams's mind was wholly on the tape ahead, as trained by Mussabini, whose advice was 'Only think of two things – the gun and the tape.'

Athletic News set the scene for the final, describing the 'perfect silence' as the finalists 'had knelt down at the start point':

> The men got down and as the pistol cracked they rose to a beautiful start. Abrahams was slow in getting away (the previous heat he lost a yard and yet won), but at half way he was just level with Scholz and Bowman. He fought with characteristic determination. His long, raking stride, his forward body movement and beautiful arm action told its story.

The *Leeds Mercury* recalled a 'long roar of wild cheering throughout the race', as Abrahams, 'inch-by-inch . . . forged ahead, and seemed to gain half-an-inch at each stride from the half-way mark'.[126] The *Athletic News* reported:

> Twenty yards from the line he [Abrahams] was in front by a yard; three yards from the line he was a yard in front, and so he broke the worst with the distance in hand, and Scholz was his nearest opponent.[127]

The result for Abrahams was unexpected. The headline on the 8 July 2024 edition of the *Leeds Mercury* proclaimed:

> World's Records Broken. Abrahams Beats the American Stars. Two Big Jumps.

Harold Abrahams was victorious. In two days he had three times equalled the Olympic record for the 100 metres. The newspapers described him as the 'mighty Abrahams',[128] 'the hero of the Olympiad'[129] with a 'beautifully run race throughout'.[130] The *Leeds Mercury* reported the 'indescribable enthusiasm' the crowds had for Abrahams's victory, with the cheering lasting 'some minutes, a truly international tribute'.[131] The *Yorkshire Post and Leeds Intelligencer* noted how the American team supported the British sprinter:

The scene of enthusiasm was beyond description, by far the greatest ovation yet seen here, and to their credit be it noted that the American sprinters and the Americans in the stand joined whole-heartedly the cheering and congratulating.[132]

The *Belfast Telegraph* reported the same phenomenon, noting that the 'crack Californian sprinter' Charles Paddock was 'bubbling over with enthusiasm concerning the feats of Abrahams', and saying, 'We think your Harold Abrahams one of the most wonderful sprinters in history; in fact, we have never seen a better man in action.'[133]

And *The Sketch* agreed, writing that Abrahams could now 'claim to be the world's fastest sprinter'.[134]

Soon after the Olympics, Harold Abraham injured himself and retired from international running. By the time he died in 1976, he was a leading sports writer and broadcaster. He was considered the 'elder statesman' of British athletics, more established in society than he had ever imagined he would be when he first started out at Cambridge.

15

James Francis Thorpe
(1887/8–1953)

> He whose morals and virtues are praiseworthy
> is preferred in the presence of God.[135]

Wa-tho-huk (meaning 'Bright Path' in the Sac and Fox language), known as James Francis Thorpe, was a member of the Sac and Fox and Potawatomi Native American nations and also had Menomine, Kickapoo, Irish and French ancestry.[136] He aspired for 'one world'. From his birth in Oklahoma territory in 1888, he was branded an outsider. He grew up with the strengths of an ancient and noble people who taught him timeless qualities of good character.

In 1912 at the Games in Stockholm, Sweden he won four of the five-event pentathlon contests, including the long jump, discus throws, and two running races. He lost the javelin throw. As for the ten-event contest, the decathlon, he won that too. He was lauded in his time as the 'first true Olympic star'. His 'warrior spirit',[137] nourished by his religious and cultural background, good coaching and training, all came together for him to achieve something larger than sports alone.

At the age of 24, Thorpe made a lasting impact on national and international sports. He brought home two gold medals for the United States and was the first Native American to obtain an Olympic gold medal for the US. It is worth remembering that at this time he was not yet recognized as an American citizen:

> You have to remember, when Jim Thorpe won the gold
> medals in 1912, Native Americans were not even citizens.

As you know, that did not occur until 1924. So when he won it, Americans wanted to own him, but yet there was contempt towards him. There were some who reached out to him while at the same time rejecting him.[138]

Thorpe dominated in every sport he played. King Gustav V of Sweden, told him, 'You sir, are the greatest athlete in the world.' To which he simply replied, 'Thanks, King.'

Maybe Thorpe heard something more than royal politeness. He had struggled against open and veiled prejudices, polite condescension. Still, he manifested good qualities, even with hurt feelings. He did not feel the king was mocking him. He knew how very rare it was in America – and in other countries – for a Native American, an African-American, an immigrant from almost any European country, an African, or any other male 'outsider' to be called 'sir'. Thorpe's hopes to be hailed as a person wherever he was were fulfilled at the Olympics. For in those Games striving mightily with confidence and true humility could level any prejudices, any feelings of exaltations, based, for example, on class, ethnicity, skin colour or religious background. He won genuine respect and admiration.

Imagine that 'Bright Path' won Olympic gold for the spiritual enrichment of humanity by those virtues he manifested in and outside athletics matches. Ahead of his Olympic contest, his shoes and socks were stolen by a competitor. Instead of giving in, he grabbed two mismatched shoes, one from a trash can, and went on to win gold. A picture of Thorpe after his Olympic win shows him wearing mismatched shoes and socks.[139]

About six months later Thorpe's medals were taken away after it was discovered that he'd been paid for playing semi-professional baseball. The International Olympic Committee (IOC) ruled that this made him a professional athlete. Only amateurs – unpaid athletes – were allowed to participate in the Olympics at that time. He was heartbroken. Thorpe wrote a letter to officials explaining that he didn't know he was doing anything wrong. He wasn't trying to hide anything. The officials didn't accept his explanation.

JAMES FRANCIS THORPE (1887–1953)

Jim Thorpe with mismatched shoes and socks

Thirty years after his death, a petition carrying one million signatures called for a reversal of the decision by the IOC that had 'cheated Jim Thorpe out of his Olympic wins'. His medals were returned by the IOC to his daughter in 1983. His name was put back in the record book 'where it belonged'. However, his status as the winner was not admitted, until Friday, 15 July 2022 when he was 'reinstated by the Olympic Committee as the winner of the 1912 Olympic pentathlon and decathlon in Stockholm, more than a century after he was stripped of his gold medals . . . the International Olympic Committee declared Thorpe the winner of the events, which coincided with the 110th anniversary of his decathlon win' when King Gustav V proclaimed him 'the greatest athlete in the world'.[140]

Thorpe always competed for a higher purpose. He kept going for the gold of helping others, putting others before himself. As he did in athletics, he gave his all when caring for his people. He earned the nickname 'Akapamata', meaning 'Caregiver' in the Sac and Fox language, for tirelessly helping his fellow Native Americans to obtain jobs and care. Many who knew him said he taught that 'whatever you're after, keep going'.[141]

It appears he was among those 'great ones' his peoples dreamed would do mightily. It is known for certain that all Thorpe's peoples are embraced in the Bahá'í teachings about human oneness: 'You must attach great importance', 'Abdu'l-Bahá urged the Bahá'ís, to 'the original inhabitants of America . . . there can be no doubt that through the Divine teachings they will become so enlightened that the whole earth will be illumined.'[142]

16
Betty Robinson (1911–99) and Other Pioneers

Speaking of James Thorpe's stolen shoes, when Betty Robinson became the first female to run in track events in the 1928 Amsterdam Games, she'd brought from her American home two left shoes. At the Games she managed to find a right one and she won the 100 metre race. Robinson became the first woman to win gold in a track contest. Three years later she was in a plane crash, from which it took years to recover. But in 1936 she was back in the Olympics. She won gold again – this time as part of a winning relay team.[143]

Imagine that when Betty Robinson and Jim Thorpe found running shoes for their runs, it enhanced the togetherness theme of the Olympics. It brings to mind that old African-American spiritual:

Betty Robinson

I got shoes. You got shoes. All God's children got shoes. When I get to heaven gonna put on my shoes; I'm gonna walk all over God's Heaven, Heaven, Heaven. Everybody talkin' 'bout Heaven ain't goin' there, Heaven, Heaven; Gonna walk all over God's Heaven!

Jesse Owens

So it is, the Olympics have been a 'heaven', a higher place, that inspires hope for equality, fairness, respect, togetherness, oneness. Recall too Jesse Owens's victories for unity in Berlin 1936. He won gold medals in the 100 metres, 200 metres, the long jump and 4 x 100 metres relay. Born in a segregated American Southern city, the youngest of ten children, a schoolteacher misheard him when he said his name was 'J.C. Owens'. He was known as 'Jesse' ever after.[144]

He too called upon those deep inspirations of self-worth and overcoming that his downtrodden parents had sung into his heart:

Jesse Owens, Berlin, 1936

Sing a song full of the faith that the dark past has taught us,
Sing a song full of the hope that the present has brought us;
Facing the rising sun of our new day begun,
Let us march on till victory is won.[145]

Unity of Races

There are numerous Olympic victories like Owens's and Luz Long's which demonstrate the Games' winning ways. They show that the Olympics have always been on the right side of history. Whether athletes win medals or not, those Games 'level social differences, to make talent and ability transparent in an otherwise unjust world'.[146] Endearing stories for all built for the ages – male and female, black and white, red, and brown and yellow, 'athletes who strove for perfect equity'; who made hearts leap, who made 'eyes smile' and 'thinking expand.'[147] All illustrating that 'together' means we are all one human family. For this theme is undoubtedly a feature of that 'candle' of 'unity of races',[148] a direction for humanity, espoused in Bahá'í writings, 'making of all that dwell on earth peoples and kindreds of one race'.[149]

* * *

Charlotte Cooper

Women took part in the Olympic Games for the first time in Paris 1900. Britain's Charlotte Cooper won two gold medals. She became the first Olympic tennis champion. Katie Ledecky, an American freestyle swimmer, won her first Olympic gold medal at the 2012 Games in London at 15 years old. She has since won ten Olympic medals, seven of them gold. She has also won the Presidential Medal of Freedom, the nation's highest civilian honour, the first swimmer to receive one. One of her coaches said of her achievements, 'Ms. Ledecky, even at her elite level is coachable and teachable.' He said she was one of the humblest people he had ever met. 'I've never heard her mention she has a world record, a gold medal or a world title.'[150]

Bear in mind that some people feel that freedom from humility is not a desirable quality. Bahá'u'lláh taught:

> Know ye not why We created you all from the same dust? That no one should exalt himself over the other. Ponder at all times in your hearts how ye were created. Since We have created you all from one same substance it is incumbent on you to be even as one soul, to walk with the same feet, eat with the same mouth and dwell in the same land, that from your inmost being, by your deeds and actions, the signs of oneness and the essence of detachment may be made manifest.[151]

What a magnanimous vision, is it not, for all the ages? The glory of a soul to have striven mightily, having done the best it could – an ancient, prevailing sentiment, complex and at times elusive. It seems the emotions of those thousands upon thousands of world-class Olympic athletes who went home from the Games in 1896, and in all the Games since, without gold or silver or bronze medals cannot be readily characterized. Perhaps, many felt deep down inside themselves a gladness that their names were not only recorded in Olympic archives but written in the hearts and minds of kin and kindred, of friends and associates and admirers pleased to know an Olympian who had served the movement for world peace, for unity in diversity, the best they could.

Marion Holley Hofman

Marion Holley (1910–95), for instance, was a young US track and field athlete who competed in the 1928 Summer Olympics. It was the year in which women participated for the first time

BETTY ROBINSON (1911–99)

Marion Holley on her way to the Amsterdam Olympics, 1928, aged 18

in track and field contests. She placed ninth in the high jump contest in which she had specialized over many years.

Something is known for certain of the positive impact of her great Olympic endeavour and she maintained her love for sports. Still, it seems she searched for a higher place, somewhere she might someday stand victorious in her own spiritual aspirations for herself and for human oneness. Raised in California in a Bahá'í home, she participated in sports activities at Stanford University and beyond. She helped conduct activities for youth. She presented numerous lectures. And she wrote 'numerous articles', some at the request of Shoghi Effendi, the head of the Bahá'í Faith, who called her one of the best writers in America on the Cause when she was only 23. At the age of 28 she was appointed to the Bahá'í National Teaching Committee, responsible for inspiring and assisting Bahá'ís to share their religion with others during the seven-year period 1937–44, the first national plan of this sort. She also travelled throughout the United States as a public speaker.

In 1945, following distinguished Bahá'í activities in America, she moved to the UK to marry David Hofman who had established the publishing company George Ronald. Shoghi Effendi wrote to the British National Spiritual Assembly, the Bahá'í governing council, to draw on her experience for their own six-year Plan and she immediately began to serve on both the National Teaching Committee and the National Spiritual Assembly before being appointed in 1954 to the first board appointed to assist the growth of the Bahá'í Faith in Europe, the Auxiliary Board.

When David Hofman was elected in 1963 to the Universal House of Justice, the international governing council of the Bahá'í worldwide community, he moved to Haifa, Israel, while Marion stayed home to be nearer to their children and to manage the UK publishing company for another 12 years.

17
Prophetic Signs of Physical Valour

> He Who is everlastingly hidden
> from the eyes of men can never be known
> except through His Manifestation,
> and His Manifestation can adduce no greater proof
> of the truth of His Mission
> than the proof of His own Person.[152]

The Prophets themselves have manifested to humanity physical valour, fitness and other excellences. 'Abdu'l-Bahá has explained:

> . . . the holy, divine Manifestations have had a nature in the utmost equilibrium, the health and wholesomeness of their bodies most perfect, their constitutions endowed with physical vigour, and the outward sensations linked with the inward perceptions, working together with extraordinary momentum and coordination.[153]

A physical sign which the Báb told those who were searching for Him would note was that He was 'free from bodily deficiency'.[154] The exclamation of Quddús, one of the most distinguished early believers, upon seeing the Báb for the first time, rings with his astonishment: 'Why seek you to hide Him from Me? I can recognize Him by His gait.'[155]

Upon His exile from Baghdad in 1863, Bahá'u'lláh displayed 'masterly horsemanship'. The startled onlookers marvelled at His 'splendid horsemanship'.[156] During his ten years in the city, He had chosen to only ride a donkey.[157] Now mounted on a tall, red roan stallion of the finest breed that His followers had acquired, He demonstrated extraordinary physical strength, vigour, coordination, harmony and grace.

Krishna was a superb bowman and wrestler. Invited to the 'Festival of the Bow', a famous sports festival in which athletic prowess was publicly tested by King Kamsa, Krishna broke the royal bow. He defeated the famous wrestlers the tyrant ruler set against him. When Kamsa tried to slay Krishna with his sword, Krishna threw him to the ground. Krishna urged his followers: 'What matters is to perfect himself or herself and in this very affirmation and sincerity lies the victory.'[158]

The Prophet Muhammad was a skilled archer, swordsman and wrestler.[159] His sport activities also included horse and camel riding, spear throwing, walking, running and swimming. He possessed excellent equestrian skills.[160]

One may also recall those long and strenuous treks all the Prophets constantly undertook for the spread of their teachings. Each demonstrated remarkable physical fitness. Interesting enough, a century after the modern Games were restored in 1896, Jefferson Perez won the 20 kilometres race walk event at the 1996 Atlanta Games. He came home with the first ever Olympic medal won by an Olympian from Ecuador.[161]

18
Eric Liddell's (1902–45) Run

> He [God] maketh victorious whomsoever He pleaseth,
> through the potency of His behest.
> He is in truth the Powerful, the Almighty.[162]

By the age of 15 Eric Liddell was an outstanding athlete, described by his headmaster at Eltham College in London, George Robertson, as being 'entirely without vanity'.[163] In 1924 he was chosen for the British Olympic team for the Paris Olympics.

The son of missionaries to China, where he was born, Liddell was a devout Christian and a man of principle. In 1920 he went to Edinburgh University to study pure science, with rugby and running figuring largely in his life, gaining him a place in the Scotland national rugby union team and scoring many wins. His ambition seemed to be to get his degree, to play rugby and to continue working for his church's mission in China. It was his running skills, however, that won Liddell a place on the British Olympic team headed for the 1924 Paris Olympic Games. He trained for the 100 metre race, which was his best event.

Liddell learned that initial heats for his 100 metre race were scheduled for Sunday, his Sabbath day. He was favoured to win the gold medal but had to qualify for the finals, which meant taking part in the heats and winning. Yet he was firm in his convictions and remained true to his faith, refusing to run any race on the Sabbath.

The Paris Olympics opened on 5 July 1924 and on the same day the *Leeds Mercury* described the British team's 'Chances':

Liddell, a product of Edinburgh University, is leaving the 100 metres to Abrahams, and has entered for the 200 and 400 metres. His style of running is not above criticism – he carries his head too high – but a fortnight ago he ran 440 yards in 49.54 sec, time good enough to carry him into the very first flight.[164]

On 7 July Harold Abrahams competed in the 100 metre final, taking the gold. On 9 July Liddell ran the 200 metres along with teammate Harold Abrahams. Liddell came in third, winning a bronze medal, while Abrahams finished sixth.

Liddell competed in the 400 metre final on 11 July. The next day the *Shields Daily News* described the event: pipers of the Cameron Highlanders playing in Colombes Stadium just before the 'thrilling final'.

> There was a gasp of astonishment when Eric Liddell, one of the most popular athletes at Colombes, was seen to be a clear three yards ahead of the field at the half-distance. Nearing the tape Fitch and Butler strained every nerve and muscle to overtake him, but could make absolutely no impression on the inspired Scot.
>
> With twenty yards to go Fitch seemed to gain a fraction, but Liddell appeared to sense the American, and with head thrown back and chin thrust out in his usual style he flashed past the tape to win what was probably so far the greatest victory of the meeting. Certainly there has not been a more popular win. The crowd went into a frenzy of enthusiasm.[165]

Liddell was feted on his return to Edinburgh, where he graduated from university on 17 July. The *Illustrated Sporting and Dramatic News* reported that the champion was 'chaired' – carried in a chair – to 'St. Giles Cathedral, where the graduation service was held.'[166]

On 18 July Liddell was entertained at the first of a number of celebratory dinners. The *Dundee Courier* related that Lord Sands would preside over the dinner, which was

Eric Liddell at the British Empire versus United States of America Games Stamford Bridge, London Saturday 19 July 1924

. . . proposed to welcome our brilliant young athlete, Mr. Eric H. Liddell, on his return to the city from the Olympic Games in Paris, and to express the widespread admiration for his remarkable athletic achievements, and also for his devotion to principle in this connection as a reverend upholder of the Christian Sabbath.[167]

Liddell's faithfulness to his Christian beliefs was again remarked upon by the Reverend Doctor James Black, who said at a service held at St George's United Free Church:

> I would just take young Eric Liddell. It took real grit to make the stand which Liddell did, out of the fullness of his convictions, for the reverence and the sanctity of the Lord's Day.[168]

Eric Liddell remained humble through it all. In response to a request for a speech, Liddell replied:

Over the entrance to the University of Pennsylvania there are these words: 'In the dust of defeat as well as in the laurel of victory there is glory to be found if one has done his best.'[169]

19
The Unity of Mankind Will Be Achieved

The Baháʼí writings explain:

> In cycles gone by, though harmony was established, yet, owing to the absence of means, the unity of all mankind could not have been achieved. Continents remained widely divided, nay even among the peoples of one and the same continent association and interchange of thought were well nigh impossible. Consequently intercourse, understanding and unity amongst all the peoples and kindreds of the earth were unattainable. In this day, however, means of communication have multiplied, and the five continents of the earth have virtually merged into one. And for everyone it is now easy to travel to any land, to associate and exchange views with its peoples, and to become familiar, through publications, with the conditions, the religious beliefs and the thoughts of all men. In like manner all the members of the human family, whether peoples or governments, cities or villages, have become increasingly interdependent . . . Hence the unity of all mankind can in this day be achieved. Verily this is none other but one of the wonders of this wondrous age . . . Eventually it will be seen how bright its candles [of unity] will burn in the assemblage of man.[170]

The Baháʼí writings emphasize that the emerging unity of nations implies that 'national rivalries, hatreds, and intrigues will cease, and racial animosity and prejudice will be replaced by racial amity, understanding and cooperation'.[171] Baháʼís believe that this 'unity' will be fully achieved, 'inasmuch as the power of the Kingdom of God will aid and assist in' its 'realization'.[172]

As mentioned earlier, the modern Olympics, founded in 1896, were inspired by the French nobleman Baron Pierre de Coubertin, who believed that the Olympic Games of ancient Greek embodied 'the noble and chivalrous character of athletics' and therefore should be revived in all their glory. But the Baron understood that modern international sporting events could not be free of politics. He warned therefore that 'Athletics can occasion the most noble passions or the most vile'.[173] Still, he envisioned, 'O sport you are justice! The perfect equity that men strive for in vain in their social institutions rises around you of its own accord. O sport you are joy! . . . Thoughts stretched out on a brighter clearer horizon.'[174]

H.C. Baldry has observed in his work *The Unity of Mankind in Greek Thought*: 'in our own day, human unity is generally seen as a practical problem. We take it a self-evident fact . . . the human race [is] a distinct species. . .' He found that 'most of us draw the inference that between . . . *homo sapiens* there is some sort of kinship or fellowship which should influence their behaviour toward each other. 'One world', 'the human community', 'the brotherhood of man' are 'phrases on everybody's lips, and their theoretical validity is hardly called in question.' 'The critical issue,' as he saw it was 'the gap between theory and practice; the paradox of a human race acknowledging in theory to be a single family, yet split by divisions of creed and colour which threaten its destruction.'[175]

20

Practical Measures for Human Oneness

> Every believer, as the promulgator of Bahá'u'lláh's
> central principle of the oneness of humanity,
> should deeply meditate upon it and
> weigh its demanding implications
> for the profound alteration of thought and
> action required at this time.[176]

The 'foundational features' [of a new world order] were 'prescribed by Bahá'u'lláh' and are a 'commitment to the practical realization of the oneness of humanity . . . and the advancement of a world civilization'.[177]

> The bedrock of a strategy that can engage the world's population in assuming responsibility for its collective destiny must be the consciousness of the oneness of humankind. Deceptively simple in popular discourse, the concept that humanity constitutes a single people presents fundamental challenges to the way that most of the institutions of contemporary society carry out their functions. Whether in the form of adversarial structure[s] or . . . the competitive spirit dominating so much of modern life, conflict is accepted as the mainspring of human interaction.[178]

Shoghi Effendi elucidated the interrelation between concept and practice:

> The principle of the Oneness of Mankind . . . is no mere

outburst of ignorant emotionalism or an expression of vague and pious hope . . . Its implications are deeper . . .

It represents the consummation of human evolution – an evolution that has had its earliest beginnings in the birth of family life, its subsequent development in the achievement of tribal solidarity, leading in turn to the constitution of the city-state, and expanding later into the institution of independent and sovereign nations.[179]

It calls for a wider loyalty, for a larger aspiration than any that has animated the human race . . . Its watchword is 'unity in diversity'. . .[180]

It implies, he further observed, that measures for achieving human unity would include:

> . . . the establishment of a world commonwealth in which all nations, races, creed and classes are closely and permanently united, and in which the autonomy of its state members and the personal freedom and initiative of the individuals that compose them are . . . safeguarded . . . A mechanism of world-intercommunication . . . embracing the whole planet . . . and functioning with marvellous swiftness and perfect regularity . . . A world language . . . invented or chosen from among the existing languages . . . as an auxiliary to [the] mother tongue[s]. A world script, a world literature, a uniform and universal system of currency, of weights and measures, will simplify and facilitate intercourse and understanding among the nations and races of mankind . . . science and religion, the two most potent forces in human life, will be reconciled, will cooperate and will harmoniously develop . . .
>
> National rivalries, hatreds, and intrigues will cease, and racial animosity and prejudice will be replaced by racial amity, understanding and cooperation. The causes of religious strife will be permanently removed . . . and the inordinate distinction between classes will be obliterated.

PRACTICAL MEASURES FOR HUMAN ONENESS

> The enormous energy dissipated and wasted on war . . . will be consecrated to such ends as will extend the range of human inventions and technical development, to the increase of the productivity of mankind, to the extermination of disease, to the extension of scientific research, to the raising of the standard of physical health, to the sharpening and refinement of the human brain . . . to the prolongation of human life, and to the furtherance of any other agency that can stimulate the intellectual, the moral, and spiritual life of the entire human race.[181]

On the theme of the oneness of humanity and the practical measures to be taken towards its realization, it is important to mention three developments in the inclusiveness of the Olympic movement.

First, the Paralympic Games. Now the largest global sporting event for athletes with disabilities, the Paralympic Games had modest beginnings. Dr Ludwig Guttman, who set up a spinal injuries centre at Stoke Mandeville Hospital in England after the second world war, organized a competition for wheelchair athletes on 29 July 1948, the day of the Opening Ceremony of the London 1948 Olympic Games. Sixteen injured servicemen and servicewomen competed in an archery competition. Guttman named these the Stoke Mandeville Games and 12 years later, in 1960 in Rome, they opened as the Paralympic Games. They have been held every four years since then and held in the same city as the Olympic Games since 1988.[182] The 2024 Paralympic Games were held in Paris from 28 August to 8 September, with around 4,400 outstanding athletes from 184 countries competing in 22 sports and 23 disciplines for 549 medals.

Second, the creation of the Refugee Olympic Team in 2016. In March of that year, President of the IOC Thomas Bach announced its creation as 'a symbol of hope for all refugees in the world' to 'make the world better aware of the magnitude of this crisis'.[183] The Refugee Olympic Team competed for the first time at the 2016 Summer Olympics, under the Olympic

Flag. In Paris in 2024, 37 refugees – the largest cohort so far – participated in 12 sports. In the Opening Ceremony parade of athletes down the Seine, travelling behind Greece, which traditionally leads the parade of nations, the Refugee Olympic Team's boat was second of the 94 boats that carried different national delegations and received one of the biggest cheers of the evening. Nicara Shaheen, an Afghan refugee who took up her sport when she was 11 years old, explained in an interview that her motivation to participate was justice:

> The Paris Olympics will be my second time on the team. Unlike other Olympic teams, this team does not represent a country. There are 37 of us from about a dozen countries, on behalf of more than 100 million refugees around the world. Every day, I feel a responsibility to work on myself and to represent my team. There are so many negative associations with the word 'refugees'. I want to do refugees justice, and show the world that we can be an asset.[184]

Bahá'u'lláh, a refugee Himself, along with His family and fellow exiles, wrote to the Shah of Persia who had banished Him, seeking both his and God's assistance for justice and mercy:

> O King of the age! The eyes of these refugees are turned towards and fixed upon the mercy of the Most Merciful. No doubt is there whatever that these tribulations will be followed by the outpourings of a supreme mercy, and these dire adversities be succeeded by an overflowing prosperity. We fain would hope, however, that His Majesty the Shah will himself examine these matters, and bring hope to the hearts.[185]

The third of the developments in the inclusiveness of the Olympic movement is the participation of women. Women have competed with men in the modern Olympics since the 1900 Games in Paris. At that time there was a total of 997 athletes, of which 22 were women, who competed in only five sports: tennis, sailing, croquet, equestrianism and golf. For the first time in the 128 years of its existence, the Olympics Games, held in Paris in 2024, were gender equal, that is, it was the first time that 50 per cent of the athletes competing were female and 50 per cent competing were male.[186] This recalls the Bahá'í teaching that

> . . . there must be an equality of rights between men and women. Women shall receive an equal privilege of education. This will enable them to qualify and progress in all degrees of occupation and accomplishment. For the world of humanity possesses two wings: man and woman. If one wing remains incapable and defective, it will restrict the power of the other, and full flight will be impossible. Therefore, the completeness and perfection of the human world are dependent upon the equal development of these two wings.[187]

∗ ∗ ∗

Baron Coubertin declared in 1892,

> It is clear, that the telegraph, railways, the telephone, the passionate research in science, congresses and exhibitions have done more for peace than any treaty or diplomatic convention. Well, I hope that athletics will do even more.[188]

Anyone wondering whether the principle of the oneness of humanity advances the merits of the Olympic Games may appreciate that Bahá'í writings offer guidance as to what serving human oneness looks like. A great number of its millions of adherents from various socioeconomic strata, religious, national and ethnic backgrounds, share with families, friends, neighbours, classmates, co-workers, students, businessmen, farmers, labourers, tradesmen, members of all professions and occupations, tribesmen, the rich, the poor, the learned, the illiterate, the old and the young, the devout and the atheist, dweller in remote hills, the islands, teeming cities, the slums, the suburbs, their belief in the oneness of humanity.[189]

Bahá'ís around the world are striving to demonstrate that:

> The Faith of Bahá'u'lláh has assimilated, by virtue of its creative, its regulative and ennobling energies, the varied races, nationalities, creeds and classes that have . . . pledged unswerving fealty to its cause. It has changed the hearts of its adherents, burned away their prejudices, stilled their passions, exalted their conceptions, ennobled their motives, coordinated their efforts, and transformed their outlook. While preserving their patriotism and safeguarding their lesser loyalties, it has made them lovers of mankind, and the determined upholders of its best and truest interests. While maintaining intact their belief in the Divine origin of their respective religions, it has enabled them to visualize the underlying purpose of these religions, to discover their merits, to recognize their sequence, their interdependence, their wholeness and unity . . .[190]

With enlarged consciousness, Bahá'ís embrace this great truth: 'There is brotherhood intended in humanity because all are waves of one sea, leaves and fruit of one tree.'[191] Be it noted as well that 'participation in athletics is a matter within the discretion of the individual [Bahá'í], in accordance with his or her own situation, inclination, and abilities'.[192] And:

> It behoveth the people of Bahá to render the Lord victorious through the power of their utterance and to admonish the people by their goodly deeds and character, inasmuch as deeds exert greater influence than words.[193]

It is also understood that

> . . . the Spirit breathed by Bahá'u'lláh upon the world [through His teachings] . . . is manifesting itself with varying degrees of intensity through the efforts consciously

displayed by His avowed supporters and indirectly through certain humanitarian organizations . . .[194]

Bahá'u'lláh urged:

> Do not busy yourselves in your own concerns; let your thoughts be fixed upon that which will rehabilitate the fortunes of mankind and sanctify the hearts and souls of men. This can best be achieved through . . . a virtuous life and a goodly behaviour. Valiant acts will ensure the triumph of this Cause, and a saintly character will reinforce its power.[195]

21
Conclusion

Selections from Bahá'í writings offered throughout this work may be helpful in an effort to 'Consider the virtues [or principles] of the human world and realize that the oneness of humanity is the primary foundation of them all . . . Therefore unity is the essential truth of religion and, when so understood, embraces all the virtues of the human world.'[196]

Fortunately, as David Goldblatt observed, 'the Olympics continues to offer excitement, entertainment, and opportunities for reflections on its place in the world'.[197] Without doubt, the Olympic Games symbolize in a profound way acceptance of human diversity and oneness, a togetherness advanced through all its lofty activities, including, of course, those magnificent athletic contests. And whether our ardour runs to basketball, football, swimming, gymnastics, tennis, weightlifting, track, or any other sport games, hopefully a time shall come when it would not match passion for the principle of human oneness.

For as stated earlier:

> All the divine Manifestations [Prophets] have proclaimed the oneness of God and the unity of mankind. They have taught that men should love and mutually help each other in order that they might progress. Now if this conception of religion be true, its essential principle is the oneness of humanity . . . This underlies all religion, all justice. The divine purpose is that men should live in unity, concord and agreement and should love one another.[198]

So it is understood that the oneness of humanity illustrates that the 'universal fermentation' perceived

> ... in every continent of the globe and in every department of human life, be it religious, social, economic or political, is purging and reshaping humanity in anticipating of the Day when the wholeness of the human race will have been recognized and its unity established.[199]

According to Bahá'í scriptures,

> ... the principle of the Oneness of Mankind, as proclaimed by Bahá'u'lláh, carries with it no more and no less than a solemn assertion that attainment to this final stage in this stupendous [human] evolution is not only necessary but inevitable, that its realization is fast approaching, and that nothing short of a power that is born of God can succeed in establishing it.[200]

Bibliography

'Abdu'l-Bahá. *Foundations of World Unity*. Wilmette, IL: Bahá'í Publishing Trust, 1979.
— *Paris Talks*. London: Bahá'í Publishing Trust, 1995. https://www.bahai.org/library/authoritative-texts/abdul-baha/paris-talks/
— *The Promulgation of Universal Peace*. Wilmette, IL: Bahá'í Publishing Trust, 1982. https://www.bahai.org/library/authoritative-texts/abdul-baha/promulgation-universal-peace/
— *The Secret of Divine Civilization*. Wilmette, IL: Bahá'í Publishing Trust, 1990. https://www.bahai.org/library/authoritative-texts/abdul-baha/secret-divine-civilization/
— *Selections from the Writings of 'Abdu'l-Bahá*. Haifa: Bahá'í World Centre, 1978. https://www.bahai.org/library/authoritative-texts/abdul-baha/selections-writings-abdul-baha/
— *Some Answered Questions*. Haifa: Bahá'í World Centre, 2014. https://www.bahai.org/library/authoritative-texts/abdul-baha/some-answered-questions/

'Abdu'l-Bahá in London. London: Bahá'í Publishing Trust, 1987.

Athletic News, 14 July 1924. The British Newspaper Archive. https://blog.britishnewspaperarchive.co.uk/2021/07/15/exploring-the-real-chariots-of-fire/

Austin, H. Elsie, 'Matthew W. Bullock', In Memoriam, *Bahá'í World*, vol. 15, pp. 535–9.

The Báb. *Selections from the Writings of the Báb*. Haifa: Bahá'í World Centre, 1976. https://www.bahai.org/library/authoritative-texts/the-bab/selections-writings-bab/

Bach, Thomas. 'IOC launches Paris Olympics film'. June 2024. https://www.moreaboutadvertising.com/2024/06/ioc-launches-paris-olympics-film/

Bahai Scriptures: Selections from the Utterances of Baha'u'llah and Abdul Baha. Horace Holley (ed.). New York: J.J. Little and Ives, 1928.

The Bahá'í World, vol. 9 (1940–44). Wilmette, IL: Bahá'í Publishing Committee, 1945.
— vol. 15 (1968–73). Haifa: Bahá'í World Centre, 1976.

Bahá'í World Faith. Wilmette, IL: Bahá'í Publishing Trust, 2nd ed. 1976.

Bahá'u'lláh. *Gleanings from the Writings of Bahá'u'lláh*. Wilmette, IL: Bahá'í Publishing Trust, 1983. https://www.bahai.org/library/authoritative-texts/bahaullah/gleanings-writings-bahaullah/
— *The Hidden Words*. Wilmette, IL: Bahá'í Publishing Trust, 1990.
— *The Kitáb-i-Aqdas*. Haifa: Bahá'í World Centre, 1992. https://www.bahai.org/library/authoritative-texts/bahaullah/kitab-i-aqdas/
— *Kitáb-i-Íqán*. Wilmette, IL: Bahá'í Publishing Trust, 1989. https://www.bahai.org/library/authoritative-texts/bahaullah/kitab-i-iqan/
— *The Summons of the Lord of Hosts: Tablets of Bahá'u'lláh*. Haifa: Bahá'í World Centre, 2002. https://www.bahai.org/library/authoritative-texts/bahaullah/summons-lord-hosts/
— *Tablets of Bahá'u'lláh revealed after the Kitáb-i-Aqdas*. Haifa: Bahá'í World Centre, 1978. https://www.bahai.org/library/authoritative-texts/bahaullah/tablets-bahaullah/

'Bahá'u'lláh: The Divine Educator'. https://www.bahai.org/bahaullah

Baker, William Joseph. *Sports in the Western World*. Champaign, IL: University of Illinois Press, 1988.

Baldry, H. C. *The Unity of Mankind in Greek Thought*. Cambridge: Cambridge University Press, 1965.

Balyuzi, H. M. *Bahá'u'lláh: The King of Glory*. Oxford: George Ronald, 1980.

Barnes, Kiser. 'Competing for the Oneness of Humanity: The Influence of the Bahá'í Faith on the Olympic Games', *Australian Bahá'í Studies*, vol. 3, 2001.

Belfast Telegraph, 8 July 1924. The British Newspaper Archive. https://blog.britishnewspaperarchive.co.uk/2021/07/15/exploring-the-real-chariots-of-fire/

Blomfield, Lady [Sitárih Khánum; Sara Louise]. *The Chosen Highway*. Oxford: George Ronald, rpt. 2007.

Bloom, John. 'Thorpe, James Francis (1888–1953)'. The Encyclopedia of Oklahoma History and Culture. Oklahoma Historical Society. https://www.okhistory.org/publications/enc/entry?entry=TH016#:~:text=Jim%20Thorpe%20was%20perhaps%20the,as%20Irish%20and%20French%2C%20ancestry

Branch, John. ' When Art, Music and Writing Could Garner Olympic Glory'. *New York Times*, 5 May 2024, p. 1. https://static01.nyt.com/images/2024/05/05/nytfrontpage/scan.pdf

'Catherine (Cathy) Freeman (1973–)', Indigenous Australia. https://ia.anu.edu.au/biography/freeman-catherine-cathy-15410

Caughey, Ellen. *Eric Liddell: Olympian and Missionary*. Ulrichsville, OH: Barbour, 2000.

'China.org.cn', http://www.china.org.cn/sports/2021-12/27/content_77954072.htm

Christesen, Paul. 'Olympic History: From Ancient Greek Olympics to Modern Olympic Games', https://olympics.com/ioc/ancient-olympic-games/history

Corlett, John. 'Virtues Lost: Courage in Sport', *Journal of the Philosophy of Sports*, XXLLL, 1996, pp. 45–57.

Dundee Courier, 17 July 1924. The British Newspaper Archive. https://blog.britishnewspaperarchive.co.uk/2021/07/15/exploring-the-real-chariots-of-fire/

Dungy, Tony. *The Soul of a Team: A Modern-Day Fable for Winning Teamwork*. Carol Stream, IL: Tyndale Momentum, 2019.

Edinburgh Evening News. July 1924. The British Newspaper Archive. https://blog.britishnewspaperarchive.co.uk/2021/07/15/exploring-the-real-chariots-of-fire/

'Freeman, Catherine (Cathy) (1973–)'. Indigenous Australia, National Centre of Biography, Australian National University. https://ia.anu.edu.au/biography/freeman-catherine-cathy-15410/text26618

Freeman, Cathy. *Born to Run: My Story*. Camberwell, VIC, AUS: Puffin, Penguin Australia, 2007.

'#GenderEqualOlympics: Celebrating full gender parity on the field of play at Paris 2024'. https://olympics.com/ioc/news/genderequalolympics-celebrating-full-gender-parity-on-the-field-of-play-at-paris-2024

Goldblatt, David. 'The Rebirth of the Olympic Games'. Greece Is. 11 August 2016. https://www.greece-is.com/the-rebirth-of-the-olympic-games/

— *The Games: A Global History of the Olympics*. London: Macmillan, 2016.

Gusau, Murtadha. 'Prophet Muhammad (Peace Be Upon Him): The Greatest Leader Of All Times'. *Premium Times*, 30 October 2020. https://opinion.premiumtimesng.com/2020/10/30/prophet-muhammad-peace-be-upon-him-the-greatest-leader-of-all-times-by-murtadha-gusau/?tztc=1

Harjo, John. 'Warrior Spirit: Jim Thorpe's Lasting Impact on Sports'. 20 October 2023. https://www.pbs.org/native-america/blog/warrior-spirit-jim-thorpes-lasting-impact-on-sports

Herman, Gail. *What are the Summer Olympics?* New York: Random House, 2016.

Hiles, Liz. 'Jim Thorpe's Olympic medals finally reinstated after 110 years'. *West River Eagle*, 16 August 2022. https://www.westrivereagle.com/articles/jim-thorpes-olympic-medals-finally-reinstated-after-110-years/

Hufford, Deborah. 'Justice is Restored for Jim Thorpe, The Greatest Athlete in History'. Notes from the Frontier. 6 March 2021 (updated 14 January 2024). https://www.notesfromthefrontier.com/post/jim-thorpe-the-greatest-athlete-in-history

Illustrated Sporting and Dramatic News, 17 July 1924. The British Newspaper Archive. https://blog.britishnewspaperarchive.co.uk/2021/07/15/exploring-the-real-chariots-of-fire/

International Olympic Committee. 'Fundamental Principles of Olympism', Olympic Charter (in force as from 15 October 2023), no. 2. https://stillmed.olympics.com/media/Document%20Library/OlympicOrg/General/EN-Olympic-Charter.pdf

—'International Olympic Committee'. https://olympics.com/ioc/overview

— *The Story of the Olympic Games*. Olympic Foundation for Culture and Heritage. London: Welbeck Publishing Group, 2020.

Johnson, James Weldon. 'Lift Every Voice and Sing'. *poets.org*. https://poets.org/poem/lift-every-voice-and-sing

Keyser, Amber J. *Sneaker Century: A History of Athletic Shoes*. Minneapolis, MN: Twenty-First Century Books, 2015.

Khadem, Riaz. *Shoghi Effendi in Oxford*. Oxford: George Ronald, 1999.

Lights of Guidance: A Bahá'í Reference File. Compiled by Helen Hornby. New Delhi: Bahá'í Publishing Trust, 3rd ed. 1994.

'Meet Jim Thorpe, a Real-Life Native American Superhero'. https://

brightpathstrong.org/meet-jim-thorpe-a-real-life-native-american-superhero

Momen, Moojan. *Understanding Religion: A Thematic Approach.* Oxford: Oneworld, 2009 (published in 1999 as *The Phenomenon of Religion*)

Nabíl-i-A'ẓam. *The Dawn-Breakers: Nabíl's Narrative of the Early Days of the Baháʼí Revelation.* Wilmette, IL: Baháʼí Publishing Trust, 1970.

'Olympic'. https://www.olympic.com/.

Olympic Academy. https://www.ioa.org.gr/the-academy/articles-publications

'Olympic Rings: Symbol of the Olympic Movement'. https://olympics.com/ioc/olympic-rings

'Olympic Values: Excellence, Respect and Friendship'. https://olympics.com/ioc/olympic-values

'Our Olympic Chances', *Leeds Mercury*, 5 July 1924. The British Newspaper Archive. https://blog.britishnewspaperarchive.co.uk/2021/07/15/exploring-the-real-chariots-of-fire/

Porter, Catherine, and Segolene Le Stradic. 'City on Guard Prepares Olympic Opening Without Walls'. *New York Times.* 27 April 2024, p. 4. https://www.nytimes.com/2024/04/27/world/europe/paris-olympics-2024-security-opening-ceremony.html

Prebish, Charles (ed.). *Religion and Sport.* London: Greenwood Press, 1992.

The Prosperity of Humankind. A statement prepared by the Baháʼí International Community Office of Public Information, Haifa. 3 March 1995. https://www.bahai.org/library/other-literature/official-statements-commentaries/prosperity-humankind/

Rabbani, Rúḥíyyih. *The Priceless Pearl.* London: Baháʼí Publishing, 2nd edn. 2017.

Remijsen, Sofie. 'The end of the ancient Olympics and other contests: why the agonistic circuit collapsed in late antiquity'. *The Journal of Hellenic Studies*, vol. 135. Published online by Cambridge University Press 23 October 2015. https://www.cambridge.org/core/journals/journal-of-hellenic-studies/article/abs/the-end-of-the-ancient-olympics-and-other-contests-why-the-agonistic-circuit-collapsed-in-late-antiquity/CB0A74BBB381A7C9537AE62FE85CD65B

Rosen, Harold. *Founders of Faith: The Parallel Lives of God's Messengers.* Wilmette, IL: Bahá'í Publishing Trust, 2010.

Shields Daily News, 12 July 1924. The British Newspaper Archive. https://blog.britishnewspaperarchive.co.uk/2021/07/15/exploring-the-real-chariots-of-fire/

Shoghi Effendi. *The Advent of Divine Justice.* Wilmette, IL: Bahá'í Publishing Trust, 1990. https://www.bahai.org/library/authoritative-texts/shoghi-effendi/advent-divine-justice/

— (Shawki Rabbani) 'Function of Sports in Life'. *The Student Union Gazette*, pp. 28–30. American University of Beirut, 1914–15.

— Letter written on behalf of Shoghi Effendi to the Bahá'í Youth of Lima, Peru, 17 November 1945, in *Lights of Guidance*, p. 425.

— *God Passes By.* Wilmette, IL: Bahá'í Publishing Trust, rev. ed. 1995. https://www.bahai.org/library/authoritative-texts/shoghi-effendi/god-passes-by/

— *The World Order of Bahá'u'lláh.* Wilmette, IL: Bahá'í Publishing Trust, 1991. https://www.bahai.org/library/authoritative-texts/shoghi-effendi/world-order-bahaullah/

Silance, Luc. 'Symbolism in Olympism-Symbolism in Art'. International Olympic Academy, 26 Session, 1986.

The Sketch, 8 July 1924. The British Newspaper Archive. https://blog.britishnewspaperarchive.co.uk/2021/07/15/exploring-the-real-chariots-of-fire/

Smith, Houston. *The World's Religions.* San Francisco, CA: HarperOne, 2nd ed. ed. 2009.

Trunsky, Andrew. 'Beneath a Freestyler's Tranquil Surface'. *New York Times*, 9 June 2024, p. 10.

The Universal House of Justice.

Letters to:

All National Spiritual Assemblies, 31 October 1967, in Universal House of Justice, *Messages from the Universal House of Justice, 1963–1986.*

The Bahá'ís of the World, 25 March 2007 https://www.bahai.org/library/authoritative-texts/search?q=2007#s=messages-universal-house-justice

The Bahá'ís of the United States, 22 July 2020. https://www.bahai.org/library/authoritative-texts/

search?q=2007#s=messages-universal-house-justice

The Conference of the Continental Counsellors, 28 December 2010. https://www.bahai.org/library/authoritative-texts/search?q=2010#s=messages-universal-house-justice

An individual, 25 August 1994.

National Spiritual Assembly of Uganda and Central Africa. 19 August 1965, in *Lights of Guidance*, p. 609)

The Peoples of the World, October 1985 (also published as *The Promise of World Peace*). https://www.bahai.org/library/authoritative-texts/the-universal-house-of-justice/messages/19851001_001/1#830641396

The President of Brazil on the Occasion of the Opening of 2014 World Cup, 6 June 2014. http://dl.bahai.org/bwns/assets/documentlibrary/Message%20From%20The%20Universal%20House%20of%20Justice.pdf

Messages from the Universal House of Justice 1963–1986: The Third Epoch of the Formative Age. Wilmette, IL: Bahá'í Publishing Trust, 1996. https://www.bahai.org/library/authoritative-texts/the-universal-house-of-justice/muhj-1963-1986/

The Promise of World Peace. Haifa: Bahá'í World Centre, 1985. https://www.bahai.org/library/authoritative-texts/the-universal-house-of-justice/messages/#19851001_001

Riḍván Message to the Bahá'ís of the World 2008: https://www.bahai.org/library/authoritative-texts/search?q=2008#s=messages-universal-house-justice

— 2013: https://www.bahai.org/library/authoritative-texts/the-universal-house-of-justice/messages/20130421_001/1#692312956

— 2014: https://www.bahai.org/library/authoritative-texts/search?q=2008#s=messages-universal-house-justice

Wellspring of Guidance. Wilmette, IL: Bahá'í Publishing Trust, 1976.

Wade, Herman L. *Run From There: A Biography of Edward P. Hurt*. Tarentum, PA: Word Association Publishers, 2003.

Wertheim, L. Jon. 'Let the Games Begin'. 2024 Summer Olympic

Preview. *Sports Illustrated*, May/June 2024. https://www.discountmags.com/magazine/sports-illustrated-may-1-2024-digital/in-this-issue/59827

'What is the Olympic motto?' https://olympics.com/ioc/faq/olympic-symbol-and-identity/what-is-the-olympic-motto

'What and when is Olympic Day?' https://olympics.com/en/news/2023-olympic-day-what-when-theme

'Which Colour Represents Asia in the Olympic Rings?', https://olympics.com/en/news/which-colour-represents-asia-in-olympic-rings

'Yearender: Sports' key words from 2021'. 'China.org.cn', http://www.china.org.cn/sports/2021-12/27/content_77954072.htm

Yorkshire Post and Leeds Intelligencer, 8 July 1924. The British Newspaper Archive. https://blog.britishnewspaperarchive.co.uk/2021/07/15/exploring-the-real-chariots-of-fire/

References

1. 'Abdu'l-Bahá, *Promulgation*, no. 58. https://www.bahai.org/library/authoritative-texts/abdul-baha/promulgation-universal-peace/
2. 'Olympic Values'. https://olympics.com/ioc/olympic-values
3. Goldblatt, *The Games*, p. 1.
4. International Olympic Committee, 'Fundamental Principles of Olympism', Olympic Charter (in force as from 15 October 2023), no. 2. https://stillmed.olympics.com/media/Document%20Library/OlympicOrg/General/EN-Olympic-Charter.pdf
5. '#GenderEqualOlympics', https://olympics.com/ioc/news/genderequalolympics-celebrating-full-gender-parity-on-the-field-of-play-at-paris-2024
6. Thomas Bach, 'IOC launches Paris Olympics film', June 2024. https://www.moreaboutadvertising.com/2024/06/ioc-launches-paris-olympics-film/
7. 'Abdu'l-Bahá, *Selections*, no. 15.
8. Wertheim, 'Let the Games Begin', *Sports Illustrated*, p. 24.
9. Branch, ' When Art, Music and Writing Could Garner Olympic Glory,' *New York Times*, 5 May 2024, p. 1. https://static01.nyt.com/images/2024/05/05/nytfrontpage/scan.pdf
10. Articles of the Olympic Academy. https://www.ioa.org.gr/the-academy/articles-publications
11. See 'Olympic Rings: Symbol of the Olympic Movement', https://olympics.com/ioc/olympic-rings; 'Which Colour Represents Asia in the Olympic Rings?',

https://olympics.com/en/news/which-colour-represents-asia-in-olympic-rings; and Silance, 'Symbolism in Olympism-Symbolism in Art', pp. 116–29.

12 'Abdu'l-Bahá, *Promulgation*, no. 114.

13 'Abdu'l-Bahá, *Secret of Divine Civilization*, p. 9. https://www.bahai.org/library/authoritative-texts/abdul-baha/secret-divine-civilization/

14 'Abdu'l-Bahá, *Foundations of World Unity*, p. 94.

15 'Abdu'l-Bahá, in *Bahai Scriptures*, p. 274.

16 ibid. p. 276.

17 Bahá'u'lláh, *Tablets*, p. 173. https://www.bahai.org/library/authoritative-texts/bahaullah/tablets-bahaullah/

18 'Abdu'l-Bahá, *Promulgation*, no. 12.

19 Shoghi Effendi, *God Passes By*, pp. 216–17. https://www.bahai.org/library/authoritative-texts/shoghi-effendi/god-passes-by/

20 The Universal House of Justice, letter To the Peoples of the World, October 1985. https://www.bahai.org/library/authoritative-texts/the-universal-house-of-justice/messages/#19851001_001

21 International Olympic Committee, *The Story of the Olympic Games*, p. 9.

22 For the life of Bahá'u'lláh *see* 'Bahá'u'lláh: The Divine Educator', https://www.bahai.org/bahaullah

23 Bahá'u'lláh, *Kitáb-i-Aqdas*, para. 75. https://www.bahai.org/library/authoritative-texts/bahaullah/kitab-i-aqdas/

24 Quoted in Blomfield, *Chosen Highway*, p. 123.

25 'Abdu'l-Bahá, *Paris Talks*, p. 35. https://www.bahai.org/library/authoritative-texts/abdul-baha/paris-talks/

26 'Abdu'l-Bahá, in *'Abdu'l-Bahá in London*, p. 55.

REFERENCES

27 'Abdu'l-Bahá, *Promulgation*, no. 35.
28 Shoghi Effendi, *World Order*, pp. 41–2.
29 'Abdu'l-Bahá, *Paris Talks*, p. 31.
30 Prebish, *Religion and Sport*, p. 8.
31 Christesen, 'Olympic History', https://olympics.com/ioc/ancient-olympic-games/history
32 Momen, *Understanding Religion,* p. 433.
33 Goldblatt, *The Games*, p. 37.
34 'Abdu'l-Bahá, *Foundations of World Unity*, p. 108.
35 Smith, *World's Religions,* p. 365.
36 Momen, *Understanding Religion*, pp. 46, 5.
37 ibid. p. 73.
38 See Remijsen, 'The end of the ancient Olympics', *Journal of Hellenic Studies*, vol. 15.
39 Goldblatt, *The Games*, pp. 2–3.
40 ibid. pp. 28, 29, 31, 35, 37.
41 Goldblatt, 'The Rebirth of the Olympic Games'.
42 ibid.
43 Porter and Le Stradic. 'City on Guard Prepares Olympic Opening Without Walls'. *New York Times*. 27 April 2024, p. 4.
44 'Abdu'l-Bahá, *Promulgation*, no. 5.
45 'Abdu'l-Bahá, *Paris Talks*, p. 16.
46 ibid. p. 53.
47 'Abdu'l-Bahá, *Foundations of World Unity*, p. 84.
48 'Abdu'l-Bahá, *Secret of Divine Civilization*, p. 98.
49 From a letter written on behalf of Shoghi Effendi to the Bahá'í Youth of Lima, Peru, 17 Nov 1945.
50 Blomfield, *Chosen Highway*, p. 191.

51 ibid. p. 87.

52 Shoghi Effendi, *Advent of Divine Justice*, p. 34.

53 Shoghi Effendi (Shawki Rabbani), 'Function of Sports in Life', *Student Union Gazette* 1914–15, pp. 28–30.

54 Bahá'u'lláh, *Tablets*, p. 36.

55 Bahá'u'lláh, *Gleanings*, p. 299.

56 Khadem, *Shoghi Effendi in Oxford*, p. 102.

57 ibid. p. 103.

58 Rabbani, *Priceless Pearl*, p. 60.

59 The Universal House of Justice to the President of Brazil on the Occasion of the Opening of 2014 World Cup, 6 June 2014. http://dl.bahai.org/bwns/assets/documentlibrary/Message%20From%20The%20Universal%20House%20of%20Justice.pdf

60 Goldblatt, *The Games*, p. 3.

61 The Universal House of Justice to the Peoples of the World, October 1985 (also published as *The Promise of World Peace*). https://www.bahai.org/library/authoritative-texts/the-universal-house-of-justice/messages/19851001_001/1#830641396

62 ibid.

63 Baldry, *Unity of Mankind in Greek Thought*, pp. 52, 56.

64 ibid. p. 54.

65 Bahá'u'lláh, *Gleanings*, p. 157.

66 'What is the Olympic motto?' https://olympics.com/ioc/faq/olympic-symbol-and-identity/what-is-the-olympic-motto

67 'Yearender: Sports' key words from 2021'. 'China.org.cn', http://www.china.org.cn/sports/2021-12/27/content_77954072.htm

68 'What and when is Olympic Day?' https://olympics.com/en/news/2023-olympic-day-what-when-theme

69 'Olympic Values'. https://olympics.com/ioc/olympic-values

70 'Abdu'l-Bahá, *Paris Talks*, p. 120.

71 Bahá'u'lláh, *Summons*, p. 62.

72 The Universal House of Justice to the National Spiritual Assembly of Uganda and Central Africa, 19 Aug 1965, in *Lights of Guidance*, p. 610.

73 The Universal House of Justice, Riḍván Message 2008.

74 ibid. para. 8.

75 'Abdu'l-Bahá, *Paris Talks*, p. 16.

76 ibid.

77 The Universal House of Justice, Riḍván Message, 2024.

78 Herman, *What are the Summer Olympics?* p. 42.

79 ibid. p. 88.

80 'Abdu'l-Bahá, *Promulgation*, no. 114.

81 The Universal House of Justice to the President of Brazil on the Occasion of the Opening of 2014 World Cup, 6 June 2014.

82 ibid.

83 ibid.

84 'Abdu'l-Bahá, *Paris Talks*, p. 54.

85 The Universal House of Justice to the President of Brazil on the Occasion of the Opening of 2014 World Cup, 6 June 2014.

86 ibid.

87 The Universal House of Justice, Riḍván Message 2013. https://www.bahai.org/library/authoritative-texts/the-universal-house-of-justice/messages/20130421_001/1#692312956

88 The Universal House of Justice to the President of Brazil on the Occasion of the Opening of 2014 World Cup, 6 June 2014.

89 'Abdu'l-Bahá, *Promulgation*, no. 105.

90 Nabíl, *Dawn-Breakers*, p. 349.

91 ibid. p. 363.

92 ibid. p. 349.

93 Shoghi Effendi, *World Order*, p. 41.
94 Nabíl, *Dawn-Breakers*, see pp. 368–76.
95 Shoghi Effendi, *God Passes By*, p. 40.
96 Bahá'u'lláh, *Kitáb-i-Íqán*, p. 266, para. 251. https://www.bahai.org/library/authoritative-texts/bahaullah/kitab-i-iqan/
97 Bahá'u'lláh, *Gleanings*, p. 316.
98 'Abdu'l-Bahá, *Promulgation*, no. 56.
99 Corlett, 'Virtues Lost', *Journal of the Philosophy of Sports*, XXLLL, 1996, pp. 45–57.
100 Barnes, 'Competing for the Oneness of Humanity', *Australian Bahá'í Studies*, vol. 3, 2001, p. 20.
101 Nabíl, *Dawn-Breakers*, pp. 366–7.
102 Dungy, with Nathan Whitaker, *Soul of a Team*, pp. viii, 206, 207, 209, 211, 217.
103 Shoghi Effendi, *Advent of Divine Justice*, pp. 21–2.
104 ibid. p. 33.
105 ibid. p. 22.
106 The Universal House of Justice to the Conference of the Continental Counsellors, 28 Dec 2010. https://www.bahai.org/library/authoritative-texts/search?q=2010#s=messages-universal-house-justice
107 'Abdu'l-Bahá, *Promulgation*, no. 38.
108 Bahá'u'lláh, *Gleanings*, p. 250.
109 'Catherine (Cathy) Freeman (1973–)', Indigenous Australia. https://ia.anu.edu.au/biography/freeman-catherine-cathy-15410
110 Dwyer, 'The love and pain that inspire Cathy', *The Age*, 9 March 2006.
111 Freeman, *Born to Run*.
112 Hurt, quoted in Wade, *Run From There*, p. 111.
113 ibid.

REFERENCES

114 Wade, *Run From There*.

115 'Abdu'l-Bahá, *Paris Talks*, pp. 148–9.

116 'Accelerated Progress in Race Relations', *Bahá'í World*, vol. 9, p. 879. See also *Bahá'í World*, vol.15, pp. 535–9.

117 Austin, 'Matthew W. Bullock', *Bahá'í World*, vol. 15, pp. 535–9.

118 Goldblatt, *The Games*, p. 3.

119 'Abdu'l-Bahá, in Shoghi Effendi, *World Order*, p. 39.

120 Herman, *What are the Summer Olympics*, p. 51.

121 Shoghi Effendi, *World Order*, p. 197.

122 'Abdu'l-Bahá, *Selections*, p. 32.

123 'Abdu'l-Bahá, *Some Answered Questions*, no. 12.

124 Keyser, *Sneaker Century*.

125 *Athletic News*, 14 July 1924.

126 *Leeds Mercury*, July 1924.

127 *Athletic News*, 14 July 1924.

128 ibid.

129 ibid.

130 *Leeds Mercury*, July 1924.

131 ibid.

132 *Yorkshire Post and Leeds Intelligencer, 8 July 1924*.

133 *Belfast Telegraph, 8 July 1924*.

134 *The Sketch, 8 July 1924*.

135 'Abdu'l-Bahá, quoted in Shoghi Effendi, *Advent of Divine Justice*, p. 38.

136 Bloom, 'Thorpe'.

137 Harjo, 'Warrior Spirit', https://www.pbs.org/native-america/blog/warrior-spirit-jim-thorpes-lasting-impact-on-sports

138 Billy Mills, quoted in Hiles, 'Jim Thorpe's Olympic medals finally reinstated after 110 years'. https://www.westrivereagle.com/articles/jim-thorpes-olympic-medals-finally-reinstated-after-110-years/

139 Harjo, 'Warrior Spirit'; and Hufford, 'Justice is Restored for Jim Thorpe'. https://www.notesfromthefrontier.com/post/jim-thorpe-the-greatest-athlete-in-history

140 Hufford, 'Justice is Restored for Jim Thorpe'.

141 'Meet Jim Thorpe'. https://brightpathstrong.org/meet-jim-thorpe-a-real-life-native-american-superhero/-

142 Shoghi Effendi, *Advent of Divine Justice*, p. 55.

143 Herman, *What are the Summer Olympics?*, p. 30.

144 International Olympic Committee, *Story of the Olympic Games*, p. 37.

145 Johnson, 'Lift Every Voice and Sing'. *poets.org*. https://poets.org/poem/lift-every-voice-and-sing

146 Goldblatt, *The Games*, p. 3.

147 As envisioned by Coubertin in ibid.

148 'Abdu'l-Bahá, *Selections*, p. 32.

149 Shoghi Effendi, *World Order*, p. 39.

150 Quoted it Trunsky, 'Beneath a Freestyler's Tranquil Surface'. *New York Times*, 9 June 2024, p. 10.

151 Bahá'u'lláh, *Hidden Words*, Arabic no. 68.

152 Bahá'u'lláh, *Gleanings*, p. 49.

153 'Abdu'l-Bahá, *Tablets of the Divine Plan*, no. 10.

154 Nabíl, *Dawn-Breakers*, p. 38.

155 ibid. pp. 69–70.

156 Balyuzi, *King of Glory*, p. 176.

157 ibid.

REFERENCES

158 Rosen, *Founders of Faith*, pp. 161, 170.

159 ibid. p. 288.

160 Gusau, 'Prophet Muhammad'. https://opinion.premiumtimesng.com/2020/10/30/prophet-muhammad-peace-be-upon-him- the-greatest-leader-of-all-times-by-murtadha-gusau/?tztc=1

161 International Olympic Committee, *Story of the Olympic Games*, p. 75.

162 The Báb, *Selections*, no. 7. https://www.bahai.org/library/authoritative-texts/the-bab/selections-writings-bab/8#657504779

163 Caughey, *Eric Liddell*, p. 43.

164 'Our Olympic Chances', *Leeds Mercury*, 5 July 1924. https://blog.britishnewspaperarchive.co.uk/2021/07/15/exploring-the-real-chariots-of-fire/

165 *Shields Daily News*, 12 July 1924. https://blog.britishnewspaperarchive.co.uk/2021/07/15/exploring-the-real-chariots-of-fire/

166 *Illustrated Sporting and Dramatic News*, 17 July 1924. https://blog.britishnewspaperarchive.co.uk/2021/07/15/exploring-the-real-chariots-of-fire/

167 *Dundee Courier*, 17 July 1924. https://blog.britishnewspaperarchive.co.uk/2021/07/15/exploring-the-real-chariots-of-fire/

168 *Edinburgh Evening News*, July 1924. https://blog.britishnewspaperarchive.co.uk/2021/07/15/exploring-the-real-chariots-of-fire/

169 *Illustrated Sporting and Dramatic News*, July 1924.

170 'Abdu'l-Bahá, *Selections*, pp. 31–2.

171 Shoghi Effendi, *World Order*, pp. 39.

172 ibid.

173 Baker, *Sports in the Western World*, ch. 20.

174 Goldblatt, *The Games*, p. 3.

175 Baldry, *The Unity of Mankind in Greek Thought*, p. 1.

176 The Universal House of Justice to the Baháʼís of the World, 22 July 2020. https://www.bahai.org/library/authoritative-texts/search?q=2007#s=messages-universal-house-justice

177 The Universal House of Justice to the Baháʼís of the World, 25 March 2007. https://www.bahai.org/library/authoritative-texts/search?q=2007#s=messages-universal-house-justice

178 *Prosperity of Humankind*, part 1. https://www.bahai.org/library/other-literature/official-statements-commentaries/prosperity-humankind/

179 Shoghi Effendi, *World Order,* pp. 42–3.

180 ibid. pp. 41–2.

181 ibid. pp. 203–4.

182 'Paralympic Heritage', Buckinghamshire Council. https://www.buckinghamshire.gov.uk/culture-and-tourism/theatres/paralympic-heritage/#:~:text=In%201948%20Dr%20Guttmann%20organised,part%20in%20an%20archery%20competition

183 'IOC Refugee Olympic Team'. International Olympic Committee. https://olympics.com/ioc/refugee-olympic-team

184 Shaheen, Nicara, 'How I Became a Judoka'. *New York Times,* Sports, Sunday, 2 July 2024, p. 10.

185 Baháʼuʼlláh, *Proclamation of Baháʼuʼlláh,* p. 59.

186 'Paris 2024: The first gender-equal Olympics'. *Women in Sport.* https://womeninsport.org/

187 ʻAbduʼl-Bahá, *Promulgation,* p. 319.

188 Goldblatt, *The Games,* p. 6.

189 Based on The Universal House of Justice, 31 October 1967, in Universal House of Justice, *Messages 1963–1986,* no. 52.3.

190 Shoghi Effendi, *World Order,* p. 197.

191 ʻAbduʼl-Bahá, *Promulgation,* no. 50.

192 The Universal House of Justice to an individual, 25 August 1994.

193 Bahá'u'lláh, *Tablets*, p. 57.
194 Shoghi Effendi, *World Order*, p. 19.
195 Bahá'u'lláh, *Gleanings*, pp. 93–4.
196 'Abdu'l-Bahá, *Promulgation*, no. 12.
197 Goldblatt, *The Games*, p. 3.
198 'Abdu'l-Bahá, *Promulgation*, no. 12.
199 Shoghi Effendi, *World Order*, p. 170.
200 ibid. p. 43.

www.ingramcontent.com/pod-product-compliance
Lightning Source LLC
Chambersburg PA
CBHW060837170426
43192CB00019BA/2811